I0475292

> *"75% of applicants to our school are qualified for admissions in terms of test scores, academics, work experience, and so on. We admit the 10% who use their applications to make the most convincing arguments for why we should admit them."*
>
> –Admissions Committee, leading global business school

Contents

How to Access the AKAD Excel Worksheet

To access the free ***AKAD Excel Worksheet***, please use an internet browser to go to www.akadgroup.com. Then use the menu bar at the top of the page to navigate through "Services," "MBA," and finally, "MBA Method." From here, you should see a link to download AKAD's MBA Excel Worksheets.

If you have any trouble with the download, please contact us at info@akadgroup.com. We can simply email you the document.

The Worksheets are designed to be used with MS Excel, part of the Microsoft Office software suite. It is possible to use the worksheets without purchasing Microsoft Office by downloading the free OpenOffice software suite at www.openoffice.org, or by uploading the file into Google Docs. In either case, some graphics may not display correctly.

About AKAD Education Group

AKAD Education Group was founded by Wharton MBAs and Law School graduates committed to changing the standards and expectations in the admissions and career consulting industry by offering superior services. Our purpose is to guide and assist clients facing the complex and competitive application process to their dream schools and dream jobs.

We chose to enter this industry after observing the rapid growth of an admissions consulting industry in Asia that acts unethically and offers little value to its clients. We know that we can build a new kind of admissions consulting company that behaves ethically and measures success in terms of its clients' results. And we believe that with our unrivalled credentials and unparalleled devotion to our clients, we will become the best admissions and career consultancy in the world.

Conveying a coherent and convincing argument for admission to a competitive school or job requires the applicant to articulate very clear goals and demonstrate a high level of introspection. Such an argument for admission cannot easily be developed by merely following simple guidelines for resume writing or by focusing on strengths and weaknesses. Applicants must take a more structured and rigorous approach to planning and executing their applications. By working through such an approach, applicants not only create better applications, but first and more importantly, actually become better applicants.

We help our MBA clients become better applicants by guiding them through our proprietary *AKAD Method,* a rigorous approach to clarifying goals, communicating clearly, and developing self-understanding. We also work with each client to design a complete, tailor-made application strategy, and provide a full suite of services including guiding applicants as they write essays and resumes, choose who should write their recommendation letters, and prepare for admissions interviews.

In addition to MBA application consulting, AKAD offers the following services:

Application Consulting

- Boarding School

- University

- Master/PhD

- Law

Career Coaching

- Career Planning

- Job Hunting Skills (resume writing, interview preparation, etc.)

Companies, schools, and individuals looking for highly educated experts seek our services because we are as passionate about our clients' results as they are. To learn more about AKAD Education Group, please visit our website at www.akadgroup.com

Executive Summary

When applying for an MBA, you must first understand that the Admissions Committee (AdCom) grants admissions to the applicants who make the best argument that they will use their MBA to achieve significant and specific goals in their career and life. This means that AdCom routinely rejects smarter and more accomplished applicants in favor of applicants who make this kind of argument.

If you are an applicant, this realization may come to you as good news or bad news. If you have great GMAT scores and work at a top company, you may be discouraged to learn that these advantages by no means guarantee your admission by a top school. You still have a lot of work preparing your application ahead of you. If you have lower GMAT scores or your job has lower status than others', AdCom's preferences should come as good news: if you present a clearly argued application, you might still win a spot at a top school.

The **AKAD Method** outlined in this book takes you through the entire process of planning your application, from clarifying why you want an MBA all the way to responding to specific essay questions about topics like leadership experience or past failures. It asks you to go through challenging introspective and self-appraisal exercises to help you focus. It pushes you to evaluate yourself from AdCom's view, and think of how you can become a better applicant. It requires you to learn a new, highly structured way of thinking about your application, along with the corresponding terminology.

And yet, the **AKAD Method** also saves you a lot of time by helping you organize your application process in a highly effective way.

When you have finished the **AKAD Method,** you will not only be a much stronger applicant, but you will also be able to point to any sentence in your application and use an entirely new vocabulary to explain its specific purpose in creating an argument for your admission.

The **AKAD Method** has three major steps:

- *Application Strategy*: AdCom wants students who have a very clear set of goals and who know specifically how an MBA – not just any MBA, but an MBA from their school – will help them achieve those goals. The Application Strategy step consists of a series of introspective questions that help you choose which schools to apply to, and which lead towards the creation of a Mission Statement that details your career goals and how an MBA from each of your chosen schools would help you achieve them.

- **Communication Strategy**: AdCom expects you to show evidence of strength or of developmental potential along each of several dimensions. The Communication Strategy step helps you evaluate yourself along each of these dimensions, and to understand how AdCom will view you. The output of this section is your Admission Case, a summary of your argument for why you deserve admission.

- **Application Preparation**: AdCom expects a well-organized and beautifully written application that conveys your Admission Case. The Application Preparation step helps you carefully plan how you will reflect the pieces of your Admission Case in different parts of your application, and then provides detailed advice on how to create a resume, answer essay questions, and select recommendation letter writers. The output of this final step is a complete application that makes a convincing argument for your admission to your dream school.

In addition to the textual and graphical explanations of this guide, AKAD also provides the **AKAD Excel Worksheet**, which will help you work your way through the exercises necessary to complete the **AKAD Method**. The **AKAD Excel Worksheet** also provides a graphical summary of your strengths and weaknesses along the dimensions that AdCom cares about, so that you can develop a better understanding of your competitive position. **The AKAD Excel Worksheet** is available for free download from www.akadgroup.com. (See page 5.)

The **AKAD MBA Application Guide** is a valuable tool that will help you prepare your application on your own. AKAD also offers classroom courses and personalized consulting services to help you apply the principles of the **AKAD Method** to your application. For more information, please visit our website at www.akadgroup.com.

Introduction

Applying to Top Business Schools

So, you are considering applying to top business schools. You will be joining the hundreds of thousands of intelligent, accomplished, driven people who compete for spots in leading business schools around the world every year. With determination, hard work, a good strategy, and a little bit of luck, you may become one of the roughly 10,000 winners of this competition – those students who are annually admitted to one of the top 20 or so business schools in the world, and get a permanent leg up in terms of salary, career, networks, and social status.

As the above paragraph implies, getting in, not graduating, is the hard part of the business school competition. Once you receive a letter of acceptance (and any needed visas), it is virtually assured that you will graduate 2 years later. Business schools have near 100% graduation rates; as long as you show up for class most of the time and avoid incarceration, deportation, or death, you will graduate.

After graduation, you will be well positioned to succeed in life. You will take a job (if you don't plan to start your own company) that pays a considerably higher salary than you were receiving prior to business school, and which offers greater responsibilities and opportunities for promotion. You will have a broad command of business knowledge, ranging from hard skills like accounting and finance to soft skills like leadership and motivation. And you will be respected for having this knowledge. You will also have a strong network of relationships with classmates and other top business school students that will be invaluable to you for years to come, both personally and professionally.

The Competition for Admission, an Inside View

Let's consider the admissions process at an imaginary but emblematic top-ranked business school: American Business Center (ABC). Like most of its rival schools, ABC's school charter gives final authority for admissions to its academic faculty. However, it is rare indeed for faculty members to review any applications themselves. Instead, the faculty sets broad policies about admissions criteria, and entrusts the day-to-day admissions decision process to a permanent committee of application evaluators: the Admissions Committee (AdCom).

AdCom is extremely busy for about half of the year and much less busy for the balance of the time, so finding the right number of staff is challenging. Most universities, like ours, have staffed AdCom with as few as one permanent member for every 1,000 applicants. At ABC, we have four AdCom members. The head of our AdCom is a 35-year old ABC alumna who used to be a management consultant. She has three staff: a younger ABC graduate, a 50-year old former ABC administrator, and a 40 year-old human

development expert. During the busy season, AdCom increases its work capacity by entrusting part time staff – often students – to complete a large part of application review work.

Let us put ourselves in the shoes of this AdCom and see how the process looks to them.

Our main jobs as AdCom are to maximize the applications to our school, and then to fill ABC's class of 300 students with the best possible mix of students from among the pool of applicants. Our job performance is reviewed largely based on the number of applications we attract, the percent of admitted students who attend and graduate, and the average quality of the class. If the number of applications increases, we look good. Every time we admit a student who elects not to attend, we look bad. If simple measures of student quality like the average GMAT score and average post-graduation starting salary shift up or down, our job performance reviews follow. This creates a strong incentive for us to encourage everyone and anyone to apply (even weak candidates), and then to admit students not only based on their intrinsic qualities, but also based in part on a calculation of how likely they are to attend.

ABC Admissions Process (1)

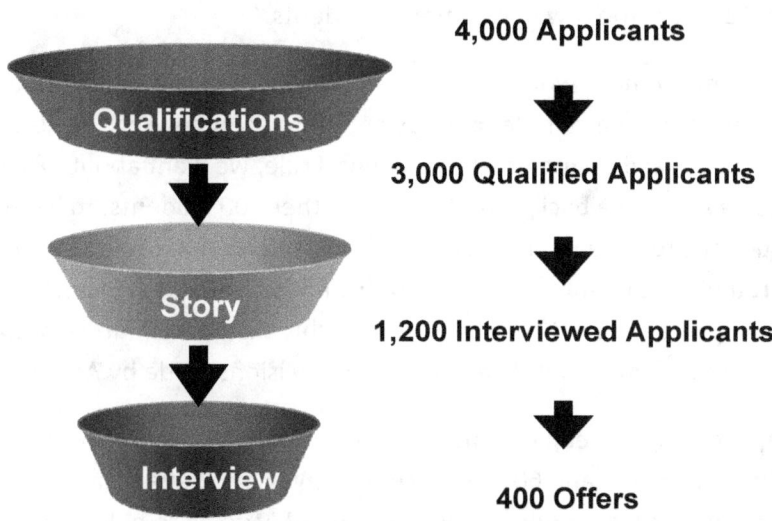

During the application season, we receive 4,000 applications – about 10 times more applications than we will eventually admit. (Because not every admitted student actually attends, we have to accept about 400 students to achieve a class size of 300. In other words, we have a *yield* of 75%.) Each of these applications has several essays, and we have to read thousands of them within a few weeks and make a decision on who to give interviews to and who to reject.

How does our review process work? Assume that ABC is fairly typical in how it structures the admissions process. On a high level, we divide the admissions process into 3 rounds: Round 1 in October, Round 2 in January, and Round 3 in March. While the overall process in each round is the same, we do have a slightly different approach to reviewing applications during each of those rounds.

During the first round we'll likely admit enough students to almost fill half our class. Remember that we have a 75% yield rate (that is, 75% of the students we admit actually accept our offer), so we will admit about 200 students in the first round with the expectation that 150 of them will accept our offer. We will do so without worrying too much about how diverse those 200 students are as a group.

However, ABC, like other leading business schools, places a priority on achieving diversity in its student body. We believe that each of our students will gain more from their education at ABC if they are challenged to work with and learn from classmates with very diverse backgrounds. So while we could easily fill our class of 300 with qualified male applicants from Ivy League undergraduate programs and leading investment banks, we don't want to do so. Instead we work actively to ensure we accept students with backgrounds that differ in many ways: ethnicity, gender, nationality, undergraduate program, work experience, etc. While ABC does not have any clear-cut requirements about exactly how many students it wants in its class from any given category, we in AdCom do have a rough idea of when we have "too many I-bankers" or "too few international students."

So while we accepted students without worrying much about class diversity during Round 1, when we get to Round 2, we are prepared to pay a little more attention to diversity. Let's focus on one dimension of diversity, career background, and assume that as a general rule, we want about 1/3 of our incoming class, or 100 students, to have finance backgrounds, 1/3, another 100 students, to have consulting backgrounds, 1/6, 50 students, to have industry backgrounds, and the final 1/6, 50 students, to have "non-traditional" backgrounds like military service, non-profit work, etc. (It is important to note that no major business school has such a clear cut "quota" system – this example is purely intended to provide a simplified illustration of the much more subtle and nuanced decisions made by AdCom.)

As we review Round 2 applicants, we keep in mind that after Round 1, 80 of the 150 students who accepted our offer are finance people and 60 are consultants. We also have 5 each of industry and non-traditional applicants. This means that in Round 2 we are probably going to hold applicants from finance backgrounds to a slightly higher standard, for fear of unbalancing our class towards finance. We might make a bit more of an effort to notice and accept good consultant applicants. And we are definitely on the lookout for applicants from industry and non-traditional backgrounds. All other things being equal, Round 2 applicants with finance backgrounds are probably going to have a slightly tougher time getting accepted than the relatively small number of industry and non-traditional applicants.

Does the fact that we might be accepting slightly fewer finance applicants during this round mean the finance applicants are bad or unqualified? No, not at all. We just don't want too many of them. If you were a financial analyst who submitted a very strong application to ABC in Round 2, you might be surprised to find yourself rejected, while a friend from another industry with a seemingly weaker application was admitted. This is a part of the luck element that is an unavoidable part of the MBA application process.

By the time Round 3 comes around, we have already handed out enough offers to fill up 275 seats – more than 90% of the class. As we review Round 3 applicants, we are looking for interesting applicants who will really round out the class in some unique way. It is tough for anyone to get into ABC during Round 3, especially for applicants without unique experiences and backgrounds.

Within a given round, how are acceptance decisions made? Let's assume that in Round 1, we receive 1,500 applications. We offer interviews by invitation only, and a successful interview is necessary to gain admission. We have the capacity to interview 300 applicants during Round 1, and will give offers to 200 of them, with the expectation that about 150 will ultimately attend.

Reviewing 1,500 applications in a few short weeks is a huge challenge for our staff. We help alleviate some of this workload by hiring "adjunct" application reviewers, as well as enlisting students to help with the reviewing work. But ultimately, at least one permanent AdCom member has to read each application. Because of our heavy workload, we are impatient with badly written or overly long applications – woe to the unwise applicant who submits essays that are poorly edited or that greatly exceed the word count limits!

> *It's not AdCom's job to admit people because they are smart, ambitious and likeable.*

As we sort through hundreds and hundreds of applications, it can become very difficult to distinguish between most applicants. The chief problem is that so many applicants describe (admittedly impressive) past achievements that all seem so similar. They are graduates of this top school or that one, some are Magna Cum Laude, some have double majors, and some have near-4.0 GPAs. They've mostly worked in well-known finance, consulting or multinational companies in almost identical roles and they've all gotten good performance reviews. Most of them have had leadership roles in some impressive-sounding extracurricular and non-profit activities. Some applicants stand out a bit from their peers because of something very unusual about their background – e.g., the woman who worked at the United Nations or the man who founded a technology company – but the vast majority of applicants seem pretty similar. Frankly, after reading 100 applications in a single week, we can't remember the difference between the 3.8 GPA Yale graduate with a 730 GMAT who worked at McKinsey and ran an ecology conference, and

the 3.5 GPA Peking University graduate with a 680 GMAT who worked at Goldman Sachs and taught math at an orphanage. We're faced with information overload.

It's wonderful and flattering that all of these highly talented young people want to come to ABC. They all seem smart, ambitious, and likeable. But it's not our job to admit people because they are smart, ambitious and, likeable. Our job is to admit people who make a clear argument that they really want to attend ABC because doing so will help them achieve some impressive and credible long term career goal. Moreover, once admitted they will make some contribution to our campus, whether simply by being actively involved in social events or via something more concrete. If they can make that argument in a way that we find convincing – and that we remember after reading 100 other applications – and if they also seem sufficiently smart, ambitious, and likeable, we'll let them in. As for all of those other applicants, even if more intelligent, more ambitious, and more likeable... well, they are just wasting their time and ours with fruitless applications.

It is also important to note that this is a partially subjective process. Part of the subjectivity is unavoidable. Perhaps one of our AdCom members really likes athletes, believing that the teamwork skills developed playing sports are important to business, while another AdCom member thinks of athletes as being rather dull-witted. If you write a great essay about the leadership skills you learned playing baseball, and your application is read by the sports-loving staffer, you have a great chance of being offered an interview. If your application lands on the desk of the sports-phobic AdCom member, you are much more likely to be rejected. This type of subjectivity is unavoidable in the type of evaluation process we at ABC use.

However, part of the subjectivity in our process is *intentional.* After all, we have AdCom members who have business backgrounds, and we have other AdCom members who have academic or HR backgrounds. In fact, ABC has intentionally chosen AdCom members with different backgrounds, who can be expected to prefer different kinds of applicants. Some individual applicants will lose out – their applications will be read by AdCom members who are disinclined to like them. Others will be lucky. ABC designed its admission process in this way to increase the diversity of the class.

But wait – isn't this unfair? There are two answers to this question. 1, Yes, just like the rest of life, this process is unfair. You are advised to apply to several schools to improve your chances of being accepted by at least one of them. And 2, well, that depends on how you define "fair." If you think at the individual level of the applicant, maybe it is unfair. If you think at the level of the institution, creating a class with a high degree of diversity is better for everyone in the class.

Later in this guide, we will discuss ways you, an applicant, can attempt to reduce the role of chance in how your application is reviewed, by writing an application that appeals to AdCom members with a range of different preferences.

ABC Admissions Process (2)

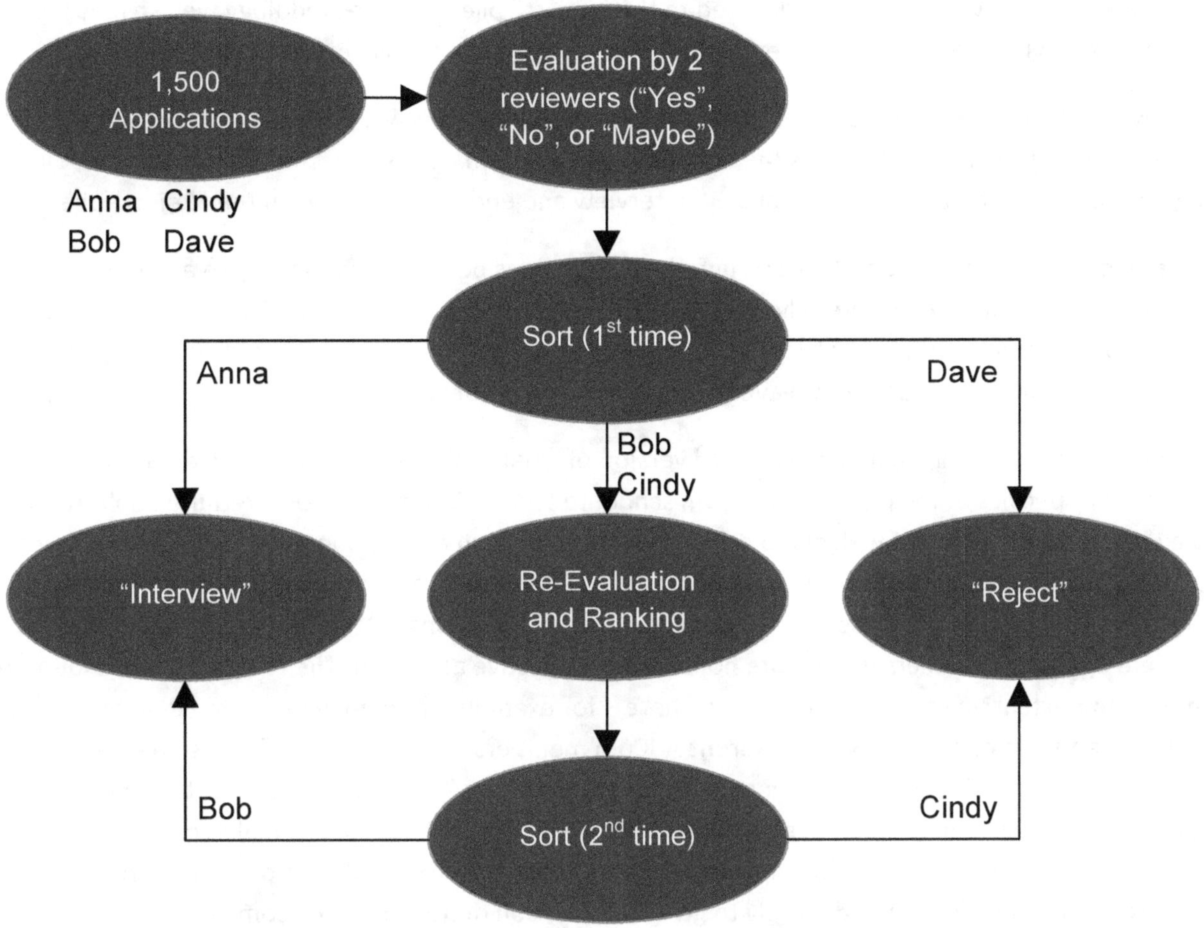

1,500
Applications

Evaluation by 2
reviewers ("Yes",
"No", or "Maybe")

Anna   Cindy
Bob   Dave

Sort (1st time)

Anna

Bob
Cindy

Dave

"Interview"

Re-Evaluation
and Ranking

"Reject"

Bob

Sort (2nd time)

Cindy

Let's follow the progress of 4 applicants through our application sorting process: Anna, Bob, Cindy and Dave. Each of their applications is read by 2 reviewers: an AdCom member and a student or adjunct reviewer. Each reviewer scores each application as "Yes," "No," or "Maybe." About 1,000 applications get scores of "No" and "No" or "Maybe" and "No." This means they are put into a "Reject" pile. Unfortunately for Dave, his application ends up here and he will soon receive a rejection letter from us. About 200 applications, including Anna's, receive two "Yes" votes, and will end up in the "Interview" pile: applications that will definitely receive an interview invitation. The remaining 300 applications, including those of Bob and Cindy, have votes of either "Yes" and "No," "Yes" and "Maybe," or "Maybe" and "Maybe." These are put into a pile for "Re-evaluation."

At this point, we have 300 applications in the "Re-evaluate" pile and 200 in the "Interview" pile. So we can move 100 "Re-evaluate" applications into the "Interview" pile to reach our maximum of 300 interviews. We use some sort of methodology to figure out which 100 applications get added to the "Interview" pile and which 200 get relegated to the "Reject" pile – the methodology we use may be a third evaluation by a senior AdCom member, a committee vote, or a discrete ranking system.

When we're done re-sorting the "Re-evaluate" pile, 300 applications will be in the "Interview" pile and 1,200 in the "Reject" pile. Bob makes the cut and his application is added to the "Interview" pile. Cindy, sadly for her, is ranked too low to get an ABC interview and ends up with Dave in the "Reject" pile.

This is an efficient method of sorting through the applications because although there are 1,500 applications, we only have to carefully weigh or rank the 300 applications in the "Re-evaluate" pile. The other 1,200 are quickly labeled as "very good" or "very bad." Of the 300 applicants who are given interviews in Round 1, about 200 will eventually receive offers of admission.

Of course, this is a simplified and generalized version of what really happens in any given B-school AdCom. The specifics of the process vary from school to school. Different schools require application reviewers to assign different weights to different aspects of each application. Some schools attempt to make the process more standardized by requiring that application reviewers assign a point score to each piece of the application and base final "Accept" or "Reject" decisions on the total point score of each complete application. Others use a more holistic and subjective approach. The real process is a lot more complex and extensive than the one depicted here – for example, there may be a good deal of discussion and negotiation between different AdCom members about which applicants receive acceptances, especially centered on those who get placed in the "Re-evaluate" pile. Oftentimes, in addition to "Accept" and "Reject," a school also may give "Waitlist" or "Conditional Acceptance" decisions to students. The above example of ABC is no more than a simplified model of the real, complex process, and is intended merely to give an indication of how many AdComs approach their job, rather than to explain exactly how the process at any given school works.

The process explained above *is* realistic in that it mirrors just how competitive the admissions process of a top business school is. Of the 1,500 applicants in our example, only 300, or 20%, are even invited to interview, and one-third of those will be rejected after the interview. These ratios are broadly in line with those at the most elite schools, though of course the exact proportions vary from school to school. This guide is intended to help you become one of the few applicants who eventually receive good news.

The Purpose of This Guide

The purpose of this guide is to help you to become a better applicant to business schools. Certainly this includes tips for improving your application: writing better essays, looking more polished in interviews, and so on. But learning how to write more clearly or shake hands more professionally ultimately will not help you if you are simply not a good applicant.

> *A good applicant knows that only after he has put a great deal of thought into his Application Strategy and Communication Strategy can he turn his attention to Application Preparation – planning and writing documents like his essays and resume.*

So, what makes a good applicant? A good applicant knows *why* she is applying to business school. She knows how she will apply specific knowledge and skills gained at business school to achieve credible, well-considered short term and long term career plans – her *Application Strategy.* A good applicant also knows *how* she can implement the application strategy to maximize the chance of getting into her dream school. She knows what points the admissions committee needs to be certain about to admit her, and how to articulate these points convincingly – her *Communication Strategy*.

A good applicant knows that only after he has put a great deal of thought into his Application Strategy and his Communication Strategy can he turn his attention to Application Preparation – planning and writing documents like his essays and resume. If he combines clear strategy early on with resolute attention to detail as he completes the application, he will be able to create a strong application – that is, not just a bunch of essays and other documents, but rather a self-contained, coherent argument to AdCom for his admission.

The Structure of This Guide

Depending on how much thought you have already put into your business school applications, you may either have a very clear and specific plan of which schools you want to attend and what kinds of courses you want to take. Or you might just have a general feeling that applying to business school might be a good thing to do at this point. In either case, this guide will take you through a disciplined and effective approach to the entire business school application process – the ***AKAD Method***.

The **AKAD Method** is a very systematic approach to planning your application, from clarifying why you want an MBA all the way to responding to specific essay questions about topics like leadership experience or past failures. It asks you to go through challenging introspective and self-appraisal exercises to help you focus. It pushes you to evaluate yourself from AdCom's view, and think of how you

can become a better applicant. It requires you to learn a new, highly structured way of thinking about your application, along with the corresponding terminology.

And yet, the **AKAD Method** also saves you a lot of time by helping you organize your application process in a highly effective way. When you have finished the **AKAD Method,** you will not only be a much stronger applicant, but you will also be able to point to any paragraph in your application and use an entirely new vocabulary to explain its specific purpose in creating an argument for your admission.

The ***AKAD Excel Worksheet,*** available for free download from www.akadgroup.com, offer a convenient, ready-to-use means of working through the AKAD Method. However, in the end it **is not the worksheets themselves, but the thought process behind them**, that is critical. Completing the worksheets without understanding the underlying methodology won't necessarily be very useful, whereas it is entirely possible to apply the methodology effectively without completing the worksheets. (See page 5 for instructions.)

The idea that will be reiterated throughout this guide is that the applicants with the most clearly developed and articulated reasons for attending business school are the ones who are usually most successful in being admitted. Therefore, the initial part of the **AKAD Method** focuses on developing an insightful *Application Strategy* that clarifies your reasons for attending business school, and your choice of school. This means reviewing your work and study experience to date, examining your career goals, determining what skills, qualities, or resources you need to attain those goals, and, finally, clarifying how you will obtain those skills, qualities, or resources by attending particular business schools.

It is quite possible that some readers of this guide will determine during this stage that, for whatever reason, business school does not make sense for them. Making such a realization early on (rather than, say, halfway through business school) will save them a lot of wasted time and money. Most readers, however, will find that going through this thought process helps them clarify their career plans and start refining their list of target schools – and at the same time, arms them with the seeds of a successful application. Remember, AdComs are on the lookout for applicants who have a clear career path and can explain how business school fits into it.

The second section of this guide focuses on developing a clear *Communication Strategy.* The fundamental basis of this strategy is marketing theory. You, the applicant, are the seller. AdCom is your customer. In order to make the sale, you need to understand what your customer wants, and then convince them that you have the necessary characteristics. And you have to do so in a way that is more convincing, compelling, coherent, and memorable than the thousands of other sellers you are competing against.

The 3 Steps of the AKAD Method

Application Strategy

- Determine needed skills and resources to achieve your long term goals
- Consider how you will get these skills and resources from B-school or other sources
- Articulate how B-school fits into your long term goals – your Mission Statement

Communication Strategy

- Understand who AdCom is and what they need to know about you before admitting you
- Form an evidence-based evaluation of yourself in AdCom's eyes
- Weave your goals and self-evaluation into a convincing argument for admission – your Admission Case

Application Preparation

- Map out your Admission Case to the components of your written application (scores, resume, essays and recommendations)
- Plan each application component with your Admission Case in mind
- Execute your application

More than anything else, AdCom wants to admit applicants it believes will attend their school if admitted, and use their MBA to become extraordinarily successful in the future. Obviously, to convince AdCom that you will attend, you need to show a lot of knowledge about and enthusiasm for their school, and to convince AdCom that you will use your MBA to succeed, you need to be able to articulate the kind of plan encapsulated in your Application Strategy. But, beyond being passionate and having a good plan, you also need to convince AdCom that you can actually execute your plan. AdCom will evaluate your ability to do so by appraising your strengths and weaknesses along several different dimensions called qualities. Section 2 of this book will introduce a framework for understanding what AdCom wants, and provide detailed descriptions of each individual quality. Then it will help you objectively evaluate yourself along each quality, and develop ways to articulate your abilities in each area to AdCom.

Once you have completed your Communication Strategy, you should be able to put together a concise argument for your own admission. Ideally, it should sound something like "My career goal is to achieve

X. I find X valuable because ... I have already demonstrated my passion for X by pursuing it in the following ways... To achieve X, I need qualities 1 to 5. I already have 1, 2 and 3, as evidenced by the following achievements... I realize I need to improve myself in 4 and 5. Your school provides the perfect way for me to do so, specifically because... I also really like your school because... And by the way, I will also contribute to the campus community in many other ways, such as..." This statement is your *Admission Case.*

When you have arrived at this type of clear Admission Case, it is time to put together your application. This is the subject of the third section of this guide, which considers the 5 basic parts of an application (academic and test scores, resume, essay, recommendations, and interview) and how you can portray your Admission Case across them to create an application that is a coherent and convincing argument to AdCom for your admission.

It is in Section 3 that this guide covers issues such as how to write an effective resume, how to polish an essay, how to choose recommenders, and so on. These are critically important considerations for any applicant, but skipping to this section without first going through a disciplined approach to planning your Application Strategy and Communication Strategy will greatly diminish the value of this guide.

Section 1: Application Strategy

Starting With Your Long Term Goals

Let us start the process of preparing for business school not by asking "Why business school?" or "What are my strengths and weaknesses?" but with a much more fundamental question: "What is my long term career goal?" Think about it for a minute. If your answer is "to be successful and make a lot of money," try thinking again. Everyone applying to business school wants to be successful and most want to make a lot of money. We need something that is a lot more specific and meaningful to you. In other words, we want to talk about something that begins to allow AdCom to see the real person behind your application. Are you replying with something such as "to be a really good management consultant?" Sorry, that's still not good enough. A lot of people want to be a good management consultant, or a great banker, or an excellent CEO. It's a pretty nonspecific goal, and because it's nonspecific, it's therefore common, which means it's boring to an AdCom member, and quite possibly even to you.

Save Time with the AKAD Excel Worksheet

In the *AKAD Excel Worksheet* available for free from www.akadgroup.com, there is a tab called "Application Strat Worksheet." You can use this tab to write in all of the parts of your application strategy that are covered below. The tab also provides prompts and explanations for some of the more detailed parts of the Application Strategy. When you are done, click on the "My Mission Statement" tab to see a simple summary of your Mission Statement. These two sheets are a simple tool to help you organize your work and save time. (See page 5 for instructions.)

We need to arrive at a goal that goes beyond a career or a title. A mere title is neither representative nor definitive of a person or a dream. We want a goal that reflects ambition, and also reflects a desire to make a lasting impact in a field that you find meaningful. We need to delve into what about your planned career is inspiring or exciting to you – the greater purpose of your career.

If you're having trouble here, try considering why you don't want to do something else. For example, if you want to be a great consultant, why don't you want to be a great banker? Why don't you want to start your own company? There must be something intrinsic about consulting that you find meaningful. (Hopefully, it's not all the late nights making PowerPoint slides.) Once you can identify and articulate what you find meaningful about your career of choice, you can start thinking about how to reposition that meaningfulness into a concrete goal.

Think to yourself about what you would truly find an exciting and rewarding goal to work towards, and to leave as your legacy. It's not "consulting" – that's merely the day-to-day content of a job. It's also not just "making partner." That's a title, and while it reflects ambition, it does not describe any lasting contribution you want to make to your field. Maybe what you truly find meaningful about consulting is the idea of contributing to high-level strategic decisions. So, it seems you're excited by corporate strategy, not by consulting itself. Consulting is just a vehicle for you to indulge in your passion for corporate strategy early in your career. Well, 10 or 20 years down the road, how do you ideally want to be pursuing your interest in corporate strategy? Running your own strategy consulting practice (as a partner)? Leading the strategy of a small company (as a CEO)? Researching and teaching corporate strategy at a leading business school (as a professor)? Any of these is a good goal in that it is meaningful to you, ambitious, and a concrete way of taking a leadership role and making a lasting impact in a field that you are excited about.

> **"I kind of like applicants who admit they aren't quite sure yet what their career goal is."**
>
> -Head of AdCom, top MBA program

How specific does your goal have to be? A highly specific goal, like "I want to use my technical expertise to start a wind-power turbine blade design shop that helps reduce the cost of green energy," is great. But let's be honest here: you're probably in your 20s or early 30s when you apply. It's pretty likely that your plans will change, and your MBA is very likely to be a driver of that change—maybe you're even applying to an MBA because you want to switch careers but aren't exactly sure where you want to end up. In this case, it might not be to your advantage to force yourself to come up with a highly specific career goal. As the head of one top MBA AdCom said to us, "I kind of like applicants who admit they aren't quite sure yet what their career goal is." This quote doesn't mean that you can have *no* plan. But it does mean you don't need to have everything worked out. A strong and authentic interest in an area of business, a willingness to learn, and a realistic understanding of the directions you are most likely to head in can constitute a career goal.

If you quickly think of a goal like this, great. If not, don't be discouraged – developing and articulating a long term goal like this is not always easy, especially if you did not happen to have an early formative experience in your youth that clarified your life's goal for you! Keep thinking and refining, over a few days or weeks. Once you have a clear goal in mind, you will need to make sure it stands up to some tough analyses. After assessing your goal, you may have to return to this step to adjust or refine your goal.

Reality check: the price of success

As you consider the kind of goal you want for yourself, it is important to perform a number of reality checks. The first issue you need to consider is: what am I willing to sacrifice to achieve this goal, and what am I not willing to sacrifice? This question is very personal and there are no right or wrong answers. Perhaps you are devoted to your religious beliefs, or you have serious hobbies that you can't imagine giving up. On the other hand, maybe you have always really loved cooking, but you're willing to sacrifice that passion in order to pursue your goal of creating a green-energy start-up company – which is likely going to require you to stay in the office late and eat take-out every day for the next decade. Maybe you have a young family. Are you (and your spouse) willing for you to devote much less time and energy to your family in order to pursue your career goals?

Pursuing an ambitious, long term goal will require you to make many sacrifices. It is advantageous on two levels for you to weigh carefully what sacrifices are necessary to achieve your goal, and whether or not you are

> ### Real World Example
>
> We worked with one applicant who had a deep interest in consulting. He devoted a lot of time to thinking about his goals. He realized his interest had arisen during his youth, when his father had been laid off after his employer made major strategic missteps. The applicant saw efficient and competent strategic thinking as the foundation for the livelihood of a company's employees, and he set as his life's goal the mission of improving the strategic thinking of the large corporations in his country. To have a strong effect on these corporations, he'd most likely have to become a senior manager or even CEO of one of them. But, his focus was not on any specific company, nor on the title of CEO, nor on the money and status he would gain from becoming a senior manager, but rather on the overarching goal of improving the strategic thinking in the boardroom to ensure stable employment for his country's workers. This is the kind of goal we want to develop and articulate for ourselves.

willing to make them. First and most importantly, you should force yourself through this kind of analysis so that you are not later surprised and embittered by the price you pay for achieving your goals, and do not fail halfway through because you realize you have other priorities. Second, remember that the purpose of all of this introspection is to help you make yourself a better business school applicant. Part of being a good applicant is demonstrating the maturity to recognize and make difficult choices. Your applications will be much more convincing if you show that you've set your career goals with reference to your other priorities, and that you have a clear idea of how you will balance these different priorities against each other.

If this analysis suggests to you that you cannot achieve your goal without sacrificing other priorities that you're simply not willing to sacrifice, it's time to go back and redefine your goal. Don't be discouraged. This process is designed to be iterative. Revising your goals to reflect reality is to your ultimate benefit.

Capability Check

All right. We know what your goal is and we are confident you can achieve it while still preserving other priorities. Now let's think about what you need to achieve your goal. This is a pretty broad question so let's break it down into three areas: *skills*, *knowledge*, and *resources*.

- **Skills:** capabilities, qualities, and abilities that must be practiced until they are innate. For example, if Bob has the unusual (but acceptable) career goal of building a chain of dance schools, skill in dancing is probably a necessary skill for him, because he's probably going to be his company's first dance instructor! Rebecca, on the other hand, wants to reform the banking industry, so she'll eventually need very strong skills in leadership and communication – and in the short run she'll probably need skills in financial analysis and model design because it is for that kind of analytical work that she'll receive her first few promotions after business school.

- **Knowledge:** information that is learned through study and referred to when evaluating, teaching or deciding. Returning to our example of Bob the dance school owner, in addition to dancing skills, he will also probably need to have a deep knowledge of dancing – what styles exist, where were they developed, how can they be taught, etc. In contrast, our bank reformer probably does not need abstract knowledge about leadership and communication; she needs to be able to perform these functions as a skill, not explain them to other people. She would, however, probably profit from detailed knowledge about different accounting regimes and cutting-edge theories about banking and finance.

- **Resources:** human, financial or other resources that you can draw upon when needed. Bob, our dance school owner, will need a lump of cash – a financial resource – to pay for the purchase and renovation of his first dance studio. It's probably not a huge amount of money, but it may not be an amount that is readily available to him right now. Our bank reformer is pursuing a goal where her own financial resources will not be critical to success, but where she will need complex international relationships with various experts and industry players – human resources – in order to succeed.

In the end, the distinction between skills, knowledge, and resources is sometimes a bit unclear. It is not a good use of your time to agonize over whether to categorize something as a skill or a form of knowledge. The three categories above are meant as references to help you think through a full range of things you need to succeed, not to drive you into taxonomic dilemmas about how to categorize those things. Leave the semantic debates to academics.

AKAD Excel Worksheet

The *AKAD Excel Worksheet* "Application Strat Worksheet" tab defines a number of types of skills, knowledge, and resources. You can use this as a guide, but it is not intended to be a complete list of what you might need to fulfill your goal (you will later see that the list provided here is almost identical to the 15 qualities discussed in Section 2.) As you begin to draw up this list, you're going to be dealing with more and more information. So if you haven't been writing down your work in the above sections, it's a good idea to start doing so now. (See Page 5.)

As you make your list, consider your education and work experience to date, plus any other major activities you've participated in. How does each of these experiences contribute to the skills, knowledge, and resources you need to achieve your goal? Looking to the future, what further skills, knowledge, and resources will you need to achieve your goal? When and in what order will you need them? The more specific your career goals and the better you understand them, the more straightforward will these questions be to answer. If you can't answer these questions, before you do anything else, you should spend time doing research and thinking until you can answer them.

Conducting a Self-Appraisal

After answering these objective questions, you will be posed with the greater challenge of answering some subjective questions about yourself: Which skills, knowledge, and resources do you already have in sufficient quantity or quality? Which ones do you still need to develop further? The more honest the introspection you undertake when answering these questions, the more complete and honest your answers will be. The more complete and honest your answers are, the better the plan and strategy you can build upon them. So take a deep look into the mirror and be honest with yourself.

Keep in mind that it is not only ok to not be perfect, but the whole point of pursuing this exercise – and of completing an MBA – is because you recognize you are not perfect and want to improve yourself. If you have trouble admitting weaknesses, keep in mind that all people – even extremely successful and famous people – have flaws. Most successful people are aware of their own flaws and either work to improve them, find ways to offset them, or rely on other people to assist them. People who refuse to

> *An inability to diagnose your own flaws is itself one of the most fatal flaws you can have. And AdCom knows it.*

acknowledge or address their own flaws tend not to succeed because they leave themselves exposed to repeated failures caused by the same old flaws. Put another way, an inability to diagnose your own flaws is itself one of the most fatal flaws you can have. And AdCom knows it.

If you go through this exercise and honestly believe you already have fully adequate levels of all the skills, knowledge and resources you need to achieve your goal, either you are delusional, or you are truly exceptional and you do not need to pursue an MBA or any other form of preparation before achieving your goal. If that's the case, put down this guide and go make it happen.

Credibility Check

In addition to considering whether you are capable of pursuing your goal, you must also consider whether this goal is credible to an outsider. If AdCom doesn't believe you will actually pursue the goal you describe to them, they are unlikely to accept you. Credibility is usually judged on the basis of your past behavior.

This section is not meant to discourage you from using an MBA as an opportunity to change careers. It is perfectly fine, for example, for a woman from a marketing background to want to use the MBA as a means of getting into corporate strategy. But she had better have an explanation as to what about corporate strategy appeals to her, and what experiences she has pursued that have allowed her to realize and explore this interest.

Let's think about credibility by thinking through an example. Let's assume you studied econometrics and chaired the "Future Bankers" club in college, and worked at an investment bank since graduation. It is credible to say you want to devote your career to bringing better risk management techniques to financial institutions because you've clearly focused your education and career on finance-related fields, which strongly suggests you are passionate about finance and truly want a career there.

It is not, however, credible for you to say you want to establish and run a non-profit organization dedicated to educating poor children in Southeast Asia. Yes, you can probably argue quite convincingly that your education and work background actually give you great skills,

> *Credibility is usually judged on the basis of your past behavior.*

knowledge and resources to help you set up a non-profit educational company. But nothing in your background supports your claim to have an interest in pursuing this goal. After all, you've dedicated your entire adult life to finance; why would you suddenly give up all that money to go set up schools in developing countries? Yes, there are MBAs who pursue this type of selfless career, but *based on your past behavior*, you certainly do not appear to be that sort of person. In this case, AdCom will likely

assume that you are trying to trick them into accepting you with a false, albeit admirable, career goal. They will chuckle, throw your application into the "reject" pile, and move on.

However, if in college, in addition to running the "Future Bankers" club, you set up a tutoring service for disadvantaged high school children, and for the past few years you have devoted your weekends to creating online educational content for free distribution in poor regions, then your goal looks more credible. You have a clearly demonstrated history of committing yourself to education for the needy. AdCom is much more likely to take you seriously.

> *If you can't think of behaviors that provide credibility to your goals, you might want to revisit your goals.*

As you think about your career goals, think about what behavior you have exhibited in the past that you can use to lend credibility to your goal. Activities you participated in rarely or tangentially do not really count here. You need to be able to list experiences where you actively pursued this interest, preferably in some sort of leadership position, as a significant commitment (i.e., if not as a full-time job, at least for several hours a week), and for an extended period of time (usually, years). If you can't think of behaviors that provide credibility to your goals, you might want to revisit your goals. For one thing, it is unlikely AdCom will believe your goals. For another thing, if till now you have not taken the initiative and effort to seriously pursue and explore your goals, perhaps you are not truly passionate about them. Maybe your goals are something pushed onto you by parental pressure, or maybe while you like the expected outcome of successfully pursuing your goals, you are not at all interested in the work necessary to achieve them, or maybe your goals are brand new and untested. It is definitely not a good idea to pursue an MBA if you have not proven to yourself that you are really passionate about the goals you claim to be pursuing. If you are lucky, you will simply be rejected everywhere you apply because your application will be unconvincing. If you are unlucky, you will somehow be accepted and attend, and end up 2 years older and a quarter million dollars poorer without having come any closer to achieving happiness.

What You've All Been Waiting for: Why Do You Want an MBA?

You have clarified your goals and figured out what you're going to have to sacrifice to achieve them. You've also catalogued the skills, knowledge, and resources you need to succeed and diagnosed in which of these areas you need to improve yourself, and you have confirmed that you have a history of behaviors that give credibility to your goals. The next step is to figure out if and how an MBA will help you make the necessary self-improvements, and also to consider what kind of MBA, and which specific program, would most suit you.

In case you do not have enough information about MBA programs to answer this question effectively, below is a brief explanation of what MBA programs do – and do not – provide.

Different kinds of MBA

The *classic* MBA is the full-time North American MBA degree, and indeed, most of the most prestigious MBA programs in the world are of this model. It consists of 2 years of full-time academic study (each academic year runs roughly from August or September through April or May), with a roughly 10- to 14-week internship experience in the summer between the 2 academic years. Typically each academic year has 2 semesters: fall and spring, though in some schools these terms will be further divided and you will have 4 quarters – which simply means you take many short courses with narrow topics instead of fewer long courses with broad topics. In your first year of study you are usually immersed in an intensive, broad-based set of mandatory courses (often called the *core curriculum*) that introduces you to all parts of a business education, from accounting to marketing to leadership and everything in between. In your second year you will likely be given a large amount of freedom to select elective courses in the pursuit of some sort of specialization, usually referred to as a *major* or *concentration*. The two full years of full-time study provide enough time for a broad but deep study of business topics with plenty of time left over for job hunting, formal extracurricular activities, and social events – which often revolve around drinking. Typical students are in their late 20s and have on average 5-7 years of full-time working experience (although there is a general trend at many schools towards accepting younger, less-experienced students).

The full-time *Euro* MBA is similar in many respects to the classic version, but usually only lasts one year. The students in these programs (which are most common in West and Central Europe) tend to be a few years older than their North American brethren and therefore are assumed to already have a command of most areas of basic business, thus requiring less time in the classroom to complete their education. Still, the culture on these campuses is often much more intense, as there is literally half as much time to complete the academic program and find a new job (and in many cases, also squeeze in an internship). Whereas students in North American programs often view their MBA as a two-year vacation from reality, students of European programs find the tempo much more like that of having a challenging job. For the most part, European programs are not as prestigious and high-profile as the best American ones, but this is changing, with schools like INSEAD and LBS seeming to enjoy stronger reputations every year.

The *executive* MBA (EMBA) is a different creature. It is intended more for mid-level to senior executives who need to round out their business knowledge than for young superstars on the fast track. EMBA programs typically have classes on evenings or weekends for about two years, and require relatively large amounts of self-study. Because of the part-time nature of the program and the fact that most students have strong family commitments (i.e., children), the campus culture of an EMBA program is not nearly as strong as that of its full-time cousins. Moreover, as many EMBA students are sponsored by

their current companies, there is a much smaller emphasis on career hunting in these programs, and internships are definitely not expected (this is changing as fewer companies are sponsoring EMBA students). Generally speaking, the status and career boost gained from an EMBA is significantly smaller than that of a full-time MBA.

For the rest of the discussion, we will primarily be considering full-time programs. Part-time EMBA programs are different in terms of culture, organization, and purpose.

Academics

Many prospective MBA applicants will be surprised to hear MBA alumni and current students tell them that "academics are the least important part of an MBA." This statement is a bit of an exaggeration, typically made to impress on the prospective applicant that there is a lot more to gain from an MBA than what is learned in a classroom, and that MBA students who focus on academic studies alone are probably missing out on much of the value of the program. Nevertheless, MBA programs are intended to systematically impart knowledge, and you can't get an MBA without going to class and taking exams.

> *Many prospective MBA applicants will be surprised to hear MBA alumni tell them that "academics are the least important part of an MBA."*

An MBA education, while confined to subjects that have direct application to business, actually covers quite a broad range of topics. Depending on your educational and work background and your future plans, you will find different parts of this education have different amounts of value to you. Also, different schools have somewhat different emphases in their education programs, either in terms of subject matter (e.g., finance vs. management) or in terms of teaching style (e.g., case method vs. lecture method). It is important to note that any MBA education spends as little time on theory or high-level concepts as possible; it is focused on imparting skills and knowledge that have an immediate and important real-world practical application. If you are interested in applying humanist philosophy to business ethics, developing new theories of macro-economic development, or debating the epistemology underlying marketing theory, business school is going to disappoint you. If you want to learn how to make a financial model to value a new business, track the dollar-for-dollar effectiveness of different marketing tactics, or supervise a team of engineers to improve the efficiency of your production plant, an MBA program will seem like home to you.

Typically, the education program at any school will include training in a mix of *hard* and *soft* subjects. *Hard* subjects are quantitative in nature, and involve right-or-wrong (or at least, better-or-worse) outcomes. Good examples are finance and accounting. Either you set up your equations to calculate the dividend yield on that bond correctly, or you are wrong. *Soft* subjects are qualitative in nature and often

the correctness of an answer is either difficult to judge in an objective manner or difficult to observe until a long period of time has passed. Examples of soft subjects are leadership and human interaction courses. If your professor describes a rebellious employee and asks you whether his manager should give him more training or fire him, there is no single right answer for you to select. Given the testosterone-driven culture of most MBA programs, hard subjects are usually received with a bit more enthusiasm and respect by the student body, but all students must go through both kinds of training.

Typical Hard Subjects

- Accounting – how to assign revenues and costs to different parts of a business during different time intervals

- Statistics – how to analyze large sets of data to find correlations and causal relationships

- Corporate Finance – how to measure and value cash flows over time

- Process Engineering – how to improve processes ranging from assembly lines to product distribution

- Marketing Management – how to judge the cost and benefits of different marketing approaches

- Micro- and Macro-Economics – how to understand the workings of the economy, at a personal level and at a societal level

Typical Soft Subjects

- Leadership – how to inspire people to work towards a common interest

- Managing People – how to set up systems to reward, promote, and train employees

- Ethics – how to weigh profit against righteousness, or weigh one ethical obligation against another. (Note that Ethics is generally treated as a soft subject with no right answers – MBA programs predominantly aim to make students aware of ethical issues rather than teach them a set of absolute ethical rules.)

- Human Interaction – how to improve the impression you give other people when interacting with them

- Creative Marketing – how to create brand images that attract consumers

- Negotiations – how to arrive at better deals by leveraging relationships and understanding the interests of your counterparty

> *Reputations can help determine which students choose to attend a given school and which companies choose to recruit there.*

Note that some schools are reputed to be excellent in certain disciplines. INSEAD is regarded as an excellent general management program. Columbia is renowned for finance. Kellogg is known for marketing, Broad for logistics, and McCombs for accounting. And so on. These reputations are only somewhat valid. For one thing, any top business school will teach all subjects well; the actual difference in quality between the general management training you'd receive at, say, Harvard and Kellogg is quite small. For another thing, the reputations might represent what the school markets itself as being good at, rather than what they really are good at. And finally, school reputations take years and years to catch up with changing realities, so reputations that were accurate 10 years ago might not reflect the reality today. For instance, Wharton has dedicated a great deal of energy to developing its entrepreneurship programs and can probably rival any program in the world in this discipline, though this is not yet fully reflected in its reputation. However accurate or inaccurate they may be, reputations are still important in that they can help determine which students choose to attend a given school and which companies choose to recruit there.

Another difference between schools is in their academic style. There are two fundamental dimensions along which an MBA program's academic style can vary: the teaching method and the learning method. There are, fundamentally, three teaching methods: classroom lecture, the case method, and real-life learning.

Classroom lecture is essentially what most of us experienced in university: large lectures, possibly reinforced by smaller group discussions led by junior professors. In the lecture method, the professor is imparting important information to the students in a largely one-way dialogue.

The *case method* is probably the single most common teaching method in business school. Students are asked to read a summary of a real-life business situation, come up with their own solutions to it, and then discuss it in class. In the case method, professors are mere facilitators, as students teach their knowledge and conclusions to each other.

The final teaching method, *real-life learning*, involves students actually going into a company or other organization and trying to manage it, develop its strategy, or otherwise apply their business acumen to it. Here, the students are taught by their own experiences in the "real world" environment. Real-life learning is generally a small part of any business school curriculum – after all, it is not easy to find companies willing to let a bunch of students come in and run their operations for a day.

In a typical business school, you will encounter a mix of teaching styles consisting mostly of lectures and cases, though the exact mix varies greatly. Harvard and Darden are renowned for entirely relying on the case method to teach all courses, and Harvard devotes considerable resources to developing huge ranges of business cases it then sells to other business schools.

In terms of learning styles, schools differ in how much relative emphasis they place on individual learning vs. group learning. **Individual learning** is probably what you experienced most in college – you need to learn the material yourself, and you will be tested and graded on your own mastery of it. While you might find it more beneficial or fun to study and prepare for exams with classmates, there is no credit given for cooperating with others.

In a **group learning** environment, you are required to complete assignments with a group of classmates, and your whole group is assigned the same grade. Moreover, in many cases, you are randomly assigned to a group and have no ability to change it. This teaching method is meant to reflect the fact that most business projects are planned and executed by small teams of executives with different areas of expertise, and the group's ability to come together and leverage each others' strengths to create the best possible group report, rather than any single individual's mastery of the project's subject matter, is what matters in the end. Most business schools have at least in part adopted a group learning model.

Relationships

Many alumni of business schools will tell you that their most valuable takeaway from business school was the personal networks they developed with other classmates. These networks take the form of informal friendships and formal networks. Informal friendships are naturally formed in the course of two years of studying, job hunting, and drinking together. Maybe these friendships will continue to be just that – friendships, with no professional component. That's fine: it's always good to have more friends. But maybe those friendships will eventually lead to professional opportunities.

Note that most business schools are hard-working, hard-playing communities. While most students are open-minded enough to try to be inclusive of those with different interests, and there are many different social spheres on any campus, you will still be limited in the friendships you can make if you do not actively participate in the chaotic campus social life. A

> *Most business schools are hard-working, hard-playing communities.*

good rule of thumb about business school is that if you're not regularly taking part at least as a spectator in group activities your mother warned you about (e.g., drinking, gambling, playing violent sports, etc.), you may not be making the most of your opportunities to forge close personal relationships with a broad range of your classmates, one of the most important aspects of your MBA education.

There are also formal networks – the alumni network that each school develops. Alumni networks can be very valuable resources for graduates – even if you don't know a potential business client or partner personally, you will have an advantage in the relationship if you can network to him through an alumni network. MBA programs realize this and actively cultivate strong alumni networks. There is an important geographic component to alumni networks – even for top schools, they tend to be stronger closer to the school, and weaker the further away you get. The alumni networks for global schools like Harvard and Wharton are extremely strong and well-developed in the Northeast USA, and a while still strong, a little weaker on the West coast of the USA and in the UK. In continental Europe they are weaker still, and in Asia, while alumni clubs still exist, they are not as active or rich as their Western cousins. For programs that are more regional in nature, like McCombs, this geographic effect is even stronger, with graduates perhaps hard-pressed to keep an alumni club running even in other parts of the USA.

Career placement

A good business school will equip you not only to find a role with more responsibility and compensation in your current industry, but to switch industries entirely, or found your own company. Indeed, career switching is one of the top reasons why people apply to business school in the first place. Most business schools begin grooming their students for intensive career searches almost the minute they arrive on campus. At certain times during your time at business school, you will find yourself spending more time on your career search than on academics. Typical rosters of career search activities include resume workshops, interview practice, business etiquette training, business dress advice, industry overviews, geographic overviews, industry club events, and on-campus company presentations. After you've been through this seemingly endless gauntlet of events, you can actually start applying for jobs.

> *Business schools begin grooming their students for intensive career searches almost the minute they arrive on campus.*

All of this activity reveals just how seriously business schools take your job placement, whether it's your summer internship or your first job after graduation. Schools are fiercely competitive in attaining the highest proportion of students with employment offers at graduation, the highest average and median compensation for alumni, and so on. This focus on employment makes sense given that the final purpose of business school is to advance students' careers.

Depending on the status of the school, it will have formal recruiting relationships with different kinds of companies. A school with a global reputation will attract large global corporations (think: investment banks, consulting shops, Fortune 500 companies, etc.), whereas a more regional school will attract recruiters from the larger regional businesses (the regional commercial bank, local manufacturers, etc.) A school's industry reputation will also largely determine the types of recruiters to be found walking

around campus – a school with a strong reputation in finance will attract more hedge fund and private equity recruiters, while a school with a reputation for technology innovation will attract companies with major R&D practices.

Recruiting relationships are quite important. A formal recruiting relationship usually means that the company will give an on-campus presentation (at which it will often provide free food and drink for attendees) about itself and the career opportunities it is offering to MBAs. It will collect resumes and conduct interviews on campus according to publicized deadlines. The nature of the work you will do and your compensation will both be clear to you before you begin applying. Most likely, there will be many alumni from your school working at the company, and their presence will undoubtedly give you an advantage when the company is evaluating applicants. It is quite easy to apply to, and relatively easy to be accepted by, a company that has a formal recruiting relationship with your MBA program.

If you want to apply to a company without a formal relationship to your school, this is still possible, but somewhat more challenging. Your school's office of career management will usually have at least one staff member assigned to help students pursue opportunities in the industry and/or geography in which you are interested. They will be able to equip you with good sources of information about your target opportunity, and will also scour alumni networks to see if they can put you in touch with any graduates who can be of particular help. But if your interests simply do not match your school's recruiting focus – say, if you are at a regional US school focused on marketing and logistics, but want to find a job in finance in Asia – the information the career office staff provides you will probably not be very valuable. Regardless of the quality of information you are provided, when no official relationship exists, it is up to you to figure out what the companies' recruiting needs are, how their recruiting schedule works, and how to submit a resume and arrange an off-campus interview.

Convergence

Regarding business school academics, alumni networks and campus culture, there is an overarching trend that suggests that differences between schools will tend to minimize: *convergence*. Around 20 years ago, different business schools really did have very different academic emphases, teaching styles, and campus cultures. Maybe school X really did teach finance much better than any other subject. And maybe it was true that school Y's reliance on individual learning meant that its students were not good team players after graduation. Each school operated in its own little universe, and it was very hard to draw the kinds of comparisons that would lead to direct competition in different disciplines. Maybe employers grumbled about school Y students' teamwork abilities, but no one could objectively prove that school Y's students lacked teamwork skills, so school Y faced no real pressure to see what its neighbors at school Z were doing differently to turn out better team players.

However, the 1990s saw the advent of published school rankings in such publications as *US News and World Report, The Wall Street Journal, The Financial Times, Business Week,* etc. In these rankings, schools were compared side by side across a number of disciplines. If school Y students were not considered good team players, school Y got a very poor score in that area compared to its rival schools. Schools have been looking over their shoulders at each other ever since.

What has followed has been a gradual but steady convergence towards similar academic and career programs. Schools like school Y that were criticized early for not developing students' teamwork skills have adopted group learning models designed to improve students' teamwork abilities. Schools that were

> *There is an overarching trend that suggests that differences between schools will tend to minimize.*

described as turning out financial geniuses with the leadership capabilities of a brick devoted resources to developing new "leadership practices" that mimicked those of schools with high scores for turning out leaders. Thus, rankings have led all business schools to address their weaknesses by studying the best practices of competing schools, thereby improving the overall quality and value of their programs. And this convergence by the schools has actually decreased the differences that the rankings were designed to highlight – though the people who make their money by publishing the rankings might not be eager to admit this fact.

Rankings: use with caution

While we're discussing rankings, it's important to emphasize that you should not take them too seriously. While rankings continue to serve the important purposes of compiling a lot of statistical information and subjective opinions about schools, and of promoting direct competition between schools, with the effect of increasing the quality of the programs at all schools, you should view their specific number rankings of individual schools in any given year with a healthy dose of skepticism. First, the formulae and subjective criteria that each ranking body uses are quite different – schools that perform very well in *The Financial Times* rankings often do relatively poorly in *The Wall Street Journal* rankings. Why? Because the two ranking systems are meant to measure different things, and because the authors are humans with different personal, subjective views of each institution. (It also seems that American authors tend to favor American schools, while European authors tend to give higher rankings to European schools.) If schools can be, and are, ranked very differently by different authorities, there's not much point in getting too obsessed by the ranking given by one particular authority – unless you go to the trouble of thoroughly understanding how and why that authority makes its ranking decisions.

Second, the ranking bodies are businesses who ultimately want to sell newspapers or magazines. They can sell more issues by reporting "sensational" or "surprising" rankings. If you take a look at rankings from the same ranking body over a few years, you will note that each year the author squeals excitedly

about how school X has "tumbled" 4 spots while school Y has "leapt" forward 5 spots. The next year, the shifts are suddenly reversed. As is suggested in point one above, it is easy to change rankings by tweaking the formulas by which you assign rankings, even if no real change in has occurred the schools themselves. The authors of the rankings certainly have an incentive to seize onto and focus on small changes at each school each year as reason for changing rankings: if the rankings never changed, no one would buy the newer versions of the rankings.

> *There's really no difference between a school ranked 4 and a school ranked 7... if your school suddenly slips several points in the rankings, the only people in the entire world who notice will be business school deans and other business school applicants.*

Finally, the ranking bodies also have a strong incentive to exaggerate minimal differences between schools. As discussed above, schools have reacted to rankings by undertaking a 20-year process of convergence, in which each school addressed its weaknesses by learning from its competitors. But the ranking bodies aren't going to be able to sell any rankings if they report that "actually there's not much difference between these schools after all." Again, they have an incentive to find and focus on differences between schools, rather than commonalities.

In the end, keep in mind that there's really no difference in quality between a school ranked 4 and a school ranked 7. (There will, however, probably be a difference between schools 4 and 17.) And no, employers do not scour the rankings every year to decide where to recruit their MBA hires. Employers already know where their favorite schools are, and they will only change their views slowly over time based on the quality of the people they hire, not on something as mercurial as rankings. If your school suddenly slips several points in the rankings, three facts will always hold true: 1) the only people in the entire world who notice will be business school deans and other business school applicants, 2) even they will forget about it in a few months, and 3) this change will have absolutely no effect on your career or happiness.

So when you are applying to schools, avoid the trap of getting too hung up on rankings. If you find yourself saying either "Oh no, my dream school was Stanford because of their entrepreneurial focus, but this year it slipped to number 6 in the *Business Week* poll – not even top 5! I better apply somewhere else instead!" or "Darn, I thought I could get into Michigan, but now that it's climbed into the top 10 ranking in *US News and World Report*, I probably can't get in there anymore. I guess I missed my chance to become a Fortune 500 CEO and I will have to become a circus clown instead." Take a deep breath, slap yourself across the face a few times if necessary, and go back to applying to Stanford or Michigan. By the time you're a first year student, the rankings will probably have "suddenly" changed again.

Beyond the rankings: choosing schools

Rankings rise and fall. School reputations within the business and academic worlds move much more slowly. Top schools are generally grouped together in terms of reputational level; these informal groupings are rough indicators of the overall relative quality and reputation of the programs. Typical terms you might find on MBA blogs are as follows:

- **Top 3:** Harvard, Stanford, and Wharton.

- **Magic 7:** Top 3, plus Booth, Columbia, Kellogg, and Sloan.

- **Top 20:** Magic 7, plus Anderson, Darden, Fuqua, Haas, Johnson, Ross, Stern, Tepper, Tuck, Yale SOM, and international schools INSEAD, IMD and LBS.

These are not rankings, but groupings – suggestions of which programs are relatively equal in reputation across all business disciplines. The differences are small. Getting into a Top 3 school requires a great application and no small amount of good luck (recall our discussion of how AdCom is set up). But getting into any Top 20 school is no less demanding. While it is dangerous to use average GMAT scores when evaluating schools (because doing so tends to lead to a misleading belief that GMAT scores determine acceptances, when in fact they serve more as an initial screening device), it might be helpful to point out that the average GMAT score of students attending the Top 3 is between 700 and 730. The average GMAT scores of students attending Top 20 schools is about 690 to 720. That's not a lot of difference; in fact, there's a lot of overlap.

> *There's not a lot of difference between students who get into Top 3 programs and Top 20 programs; in fact, there's a lot of overlap.*

How should you pick schools? Should you base your choice entirely on general reputation and your GMAT score? – "I got a 750 so I will apply to the Top 3 only," or "I have a 670 so I should give up my dreams of attending a Top 20 program and aim lower." No, that is a bad strategy. As the diagram below indicates, among the Top 20 programs, different programs tend to focus more on different areas.

Is this diagram exhaustive? Absolutely not; this diagram is a simple comparison between three broad areas of business; if your interests lie elsewhere this diagram is probably not helpful at all.

Is this diagram accurate? Well, it's probably fair to say that no representative from any MBA program would accept the placement of his school on this diagram.

So what's the purpose of this diagram? It's to illustrate how you should start thinking about your school choice. If you're interested in entrepreneurship, you should be looking at a very different set of schools,

even just within the Top 20, than you should be if you plan to pursue a career in general management or finance.

An Illustrative Pragmatic Approach to School Choice

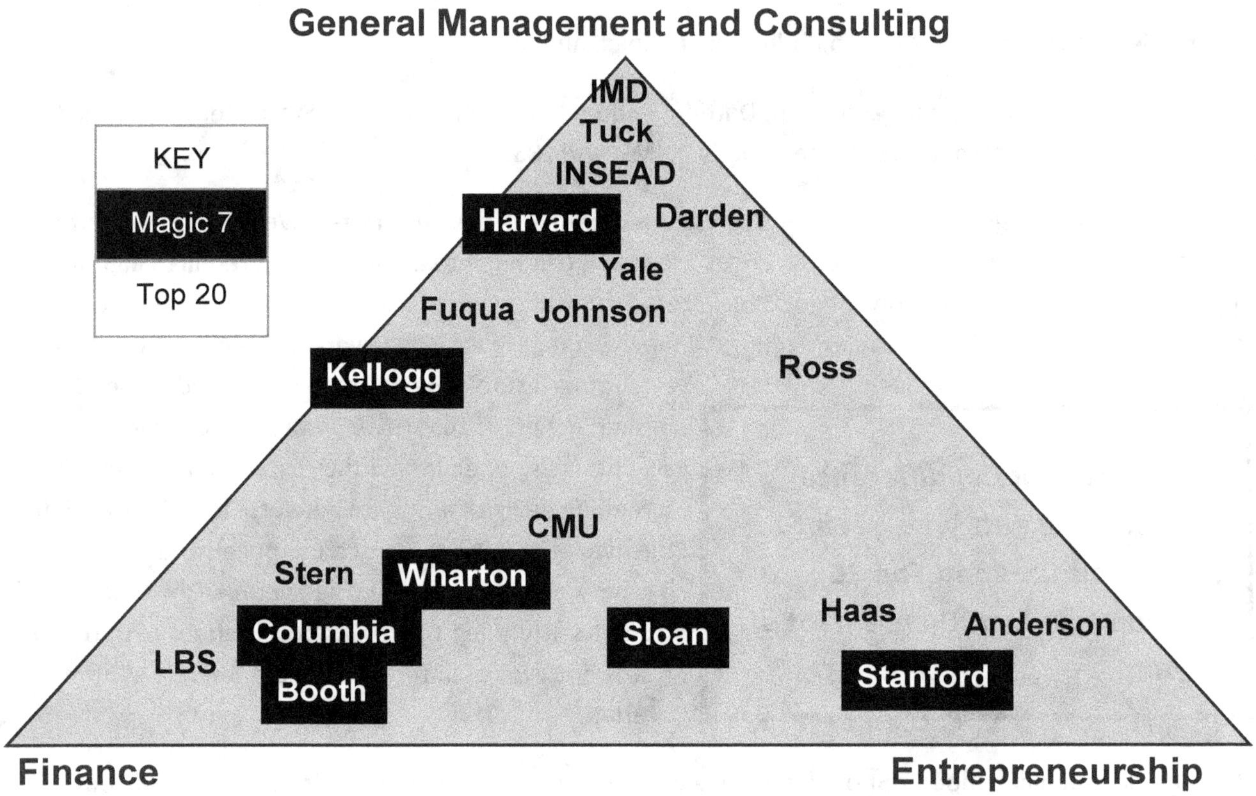

General Management and Consulting

IMD
Tuck
INSEAD
Harvard   Darden
Yale
Fuqua   Johnson
Ross

KEY
Magic 7
Top 20

Kellogg

CMU

Stern   Wharton

Columbia

LBS

Booth

Sloan

Haas   Anderson

Stanford

Finance   **Entrepreneurship**

You should base your choice of programs on what your career goal is, what you need to gain in order to achieve it, and what different programs offer. If you want to be an IT entrepreneur, it probably makes more sense for you to apply to a range of programs that fit your goals – Stanford, Haas, and Sloan, for sure, but also Olin, Marshall and McCombs (not shown in diagram) – than it does for you to simply apply to schools whose general reputation is at your "level." If you want to go into logistics, you might be surprised to learn that some of the best logistics MBA programs in the world exist at schools that are not in the general Top 20 list, like Broad and Fisher. You would arguably be hurting your professional development if you had a goal in logistics but, for reasons of status, only applied to Top 20 schools.

When choosing schools, start with your career goal. Then figure out which schools would best help you achieve the skills, knowledge and resources you need to reach that goal. Then compare your qualifications – GMAT, work experience, etc., against the averages or distributions at these schools. Keep in mind that *averages* are just that – to use the GMAT as an example again, if the median GMAT score at a school is 700, it means half the students there scored below 700, and simply knowing this average number may not tell you much about your chances if you have a 680. If possible, try to find distributions: e.g., "the mean GMAT is 700 and the standard deviation is 20." Assuming a normal distribution, this means that about 2/3 of the students were in the range of 680 to 720. As a very rough rule, if you're within one standard deviation of the mean, or within the middle 80% of scores (these ranges are often available from school websites), your chances of being accepted are ok. If you are below these ranges, you will be starting with a disadvantage. Pick a range of schools – some of which will be very hard to get into (*reach* schools), some of which you have a reasonable chance of getting into (*eye level* schools), and some of which you are quite confident of being able to attend (*safety* schools).

All of these schools should be destinations that you would be happy to attend and that would significantly help you achieve your goals. We have come across many repeat applicants who came to us and said "I was only accepted by my safety school last year, and I didn't want to go, so I decided to reject the offer and reapply to my dream schools this year." Huh? Why would you apply to safety schools that you would never actually attend? That's about as reasonable as buying a BMW and then refusing to drive it because you really wanted a Ferrari.

Take some time to think carefully about your safety schools. It is easy to identify your reach schools, because they are the ones you dream about attending. But making a good choice about safety schools requires some discipline and thought. Make sure you're confident that if you were only accepted by this school, while you might be a little disappointed, you would still be happy to attend it. Otherwise, keep looking.

> **Why would you apply to safety schools that you would never actually attend?**

You may decide that, for whatever reason, you do not want to apply to any safety schools. This is especially common among younger applicants, who figure, "if I'm not accepted by a reach school this year, I'm happy to wait another year and reapply. If that happens, then I will think about safety schools in addition to reach schools." That's a valid decision. Just be honest with yourself that you are making the choice to risk delaying your studies for a year rather than apply to safety schools.

Above, I have mentioned several times that you should do research on different schools to find out which ones appeal to you and how you compare to their typical students. How do you do so? Well, there are three great sources. The first is the rankings in sources like *BusinessWeek, Financial Times,* and

US News. While their specific number rankings in any given year should not be taken too literally, these publications do provide a wealth of information about the specializations of different programs, the profiles of typical students, post-MBA employment, and so on. Because rankings allow you to easily scan through and compare dozens of programs at once, they are a great place to start your research.

Once you have identified several potential fits, you can start utilizing the other two sources. The first of these is the official information distributed by schools – either on their websites, or in recruiting seminars they hold in major business centers. Go to their websites and look around. Attend their seminars and coffee chats. Listen carefully, and try to ask any questions you may have. Get business cards from admission officers or alumni in case you have other questions later in the process. The second of these is the informal information you can gather if you are able to talk directly to a current student or alumnus of the school. Inviting an alumnus out for coffee and asking them to talk about their MBA experience is a great way to learn about a school; you will often learn anecdotes that round out your impression of each school in a way that is hard to achieve with the statistics commonly found in rankings and from official sources. In addition, showing what lengths you have gone through to learn about the school when you are writing your application material helps to show your strong commitment to the school.

Business school costs

A final consideration about business schools is the cost of attending them. Tuition and fees at a top American school increase every year, and at the time of this writing, are approaching USD50,000 per year. And you need to pay that for two consecutive years. On top of that, you have living expenses like rent, food and drink, which might be considerably higher at school than what you pay now.

In addition to the direct costs of a business school education, there are considerable opportunity costs. Most obviously, you will not be earning salary while attending business school. It's reasonable to add lost salary to the cost of attending.

> **It's easy to arrive at a cost of over a quarter million USD.**

When you add it up, it's easy to arrive at a cost of over a quarter million USD. That's one expensive ticket. You can borrow to cover these costs. (Business school students are considered a good credit risk and can usually get financing for their entire education expense. While it's impossible to predict future interest rates, international graduates of the class of 2007 generally had loans at about 7%.) And if you're going to be applying your business school education and networks in a career in business, the costs will be relatively easy to defray. If you attend a top school, it's perfectly reasonable to expect that you will earn over $150,000 in your first year out of school. So don't let the cost deter you unless you're not sure you'll actually be gaining anything valuable from business

school, in which case the huge price tag should quickly start to concentrate your mind on other things you can do to achieve your goals.

Does Business School Have What You Need?

Consider the skills, knowledge and resources you diagnosed yourself as needing to gain to achieve your goal. Will business school help you get them? Is there a better way to get them? If business school is the best way, specifically what kind of MBA seems best suited to you – a full-time North American type MBA? An MBA at a school renowned for finance? What specific schools appeal to you most? If an MBA can provide part of the skills, knowledge, and resources you need, what steps do you need to take to obtain the remaining part?

Maybe, after going through all of this introspection and analysis, you have concluded that business school is not the best way forward for you. Maybe it's better for you to apply for an internal reassignment, or to take a job abroad, or to pursue a technical degree. Good for you – as long as you have identified a clear path to follow, you are heading towards success.

Most likely, after going through these exercises, you do believe business school is the correct next step for you. And by now, you are probably getting impatient – when are we going to get on with planning out our business school applications?

Summarizing Your Application Strategy with a Mission Statement

You know what you want to achieve during your career. You know what skills, knowledge and resources you still need to gain in order to get there. Hopefully, now you also know whether you can gain them at a business school, and even have some ideas about what kind of MBA program would be best. It is time to write all of this information down into a single, short paragraph that concisely sums up your purpose in attending business school. This paragraph will lie at the core of all applications you submit to business schools. The format of the paragraph is as follows:

(Note that the *AKAD Excel Worksheet* will automatically write this paragraph for you in the "My Mission Statement" tab, as long as you have used the "Application Strat Worksheet" tab to complete all of the sections above.)

Sample Mission Statement

In my career I want to _____. This is meaningful to me because _____. To get there I am willing to sacrifice _____, but not _____.

In my pursuit of my goal, I have already _____. These experiences have given me some of the skills, knowledge and resources I need to achieve my goal, such as _____. But I still need to develop _____.

The best way for me to obtain these skills, knowledge and resources is to pursue an MBA at _____ schools. In addition to attending business school, I will also need to_____.

Remember, making a clear Mission Statement like this will make you a better applicant. AdCom members are looking for applicants who make a convincing argument as to why they deserve admission, and the foundation of any convincing argument for admission is a clearly thought-out Mission Statement. The earlier in your application process you perfect your Mission Statement, the clearer and more convincing an argument you will be able to make throughout your application materials.

Section 2: Communication Strategy

Marketing

Now that you have figured out exactly why you want to get an MBA, and expressed that reasoning in a concise Mission Statement that can form the basis of your candidacy, it is time to begin thinking about how to make a convincing argument to AdCom that they should admit you. To do this, we will adopt some principles of marketing theory. Let us think of your application as your "product" and AdCom as your potential customer.

The purpose of marketing is not so much to *sell* a product as it is to make consumers want to *buy* the product. It's a subtle but important difference. To sell more of your product you can always cut prices, give the purchaser a kickback, open more branches or hire mobsters to shut down your competition. But in each of these cases, the consumers' view of your product's desirability has not changed – you're just giving them a financial incentive or making your product easier to obtain than competing offers. In the MBA application world, there's no "sales" focused approach to improving your candidacy (unless you have rich parents who are willing to give a multi-million dollar donation to the school of your choice, in which case you probably don't need this application guide, or for that matter, an MBA).

If you want to make people want to buy a product, you need a sophisticated "marketing" approach. That is, you need to positively alter their perception of your product so they want it more than they want competing products. To do that, you must communicate with the customer at a level and in a language the customer is amenable to. Hence, before you can effectively communicate with the customer, you need to understand who they are and what they want. If you don't understand your customer's needs, you might waste your time telling them information they don't care about or talking in a way that doesn't appeal to them.

Who is AdCom?

We already discussed this topic a bit in the introduction to this guide. But it bears repeating. Many AdCom members are *not* like you. While some AdComs are led and partially staffed by people with executive backgrounds and MBAs, who have career backgrounds and ambitions similar to yours,

> **Many AdCom members are not like you.**

many AdCom members do not fit this profile. They are *not* businesspeople. They do *not* want to become a CEO or found their own business. They probably have *not* ever worked in an analytical, planning or

executive role in a company. They do *not* read *The Wall Street Journal* daily or dream of one day having their picture on the cover of *Fortune* magazine.

Some AdCom members *might be* human resources and professional development specialists. These individuals want to contribute to the career development of talented people. They may have previously worked in human resources, training and career counseling roles. They subscribe to *Human Resources Quarterly* and they dream that someday someone pictured on the cover of *Fortune* magazine will thank them for contributing to his or her success.

Other AdCom members *might be* university administrators. These members are focused on pursuing an educational mission and on improving the status of their institutions. They are interested in smart people who want to learn. Previously they have probably worked in a variety of teaching and administrative jobs. Their ambition might be to climb the ladder of university administration and someday be thanked by an alumni conference for strengthening the university's educational reputation.

Or maybe the AdCom member who reads your application will be completely different from the examples above. It's impossible to know. This uncertainty has important implications for your application.

> *AdCom is focused on your potential to contribute and succeed in the future. Your personal qualities and past accomplishment serve as evidence of your ability to contribute and succeed in the future.*

First, your target AdCom members might speak a different language from you. While they've talked to a lot of different applicants with different business backgrounds, they may only have a spectator's knowledge of business. They probably do not understand the details of your current job – if you tell them you do "convertible bond arbitrage," they may recognize this only as "a quantitatively intense finance job"; if you say your main responsibility is "supervising network architecture in tandem with client development teams," they may very well think "ah, some tech job." Do not expect AdCom to understand any technical jargon, be familiar with the latest trends in your industry, or so on. Extending the example of convertible bond arbitrage, if you use your essays to talk about "shaving basis points off the LIBOR spread," you may confuse and thereby alienate the AdCom member who reads it. Make these points using common language that explains what you're achieving from a business, not technical perspective. Instead of "shaving basis points," you should talk about "reducing the risk premiums we had to pay." If you can't describe your work in non-technical terms, this is a strong sign that you don't understand your work, or that you're trying to create a façade of expertise to hide your insecurity.

The fact that AdCom members may not understand all aspects of all fields of business is not a reason to be patronizing to them or to treat them as intellectually inferior to you. Most quantum physicists do not have a deep understanding of business, and no one would doubt their abilities. They simply have an educational and professional orientation that differs from businesspeople's. The burden is on you to make your application understandable to an audience that is smart but that lacks the experience to immediately understand your job's content, purpose and significance.

While AdCom members have a diverse range of backgrounds and orientations, it is fair to say that AdCom is looking for the applicants who are most likely to contribute to the campus community as a student, and then use their MBA to succeed in some extraordinary way (and success is defined much more broadly than simple financial success). In other words, AdCom is focused on your potential to contribute and succeed in the future. Your personal qualities and past accomplishments serve as *evidence* of your ability to contribute and succeed in the future, as long as you present them in a way that demonstrates you possess clear goals, self-knowledge and strengths or developmental potential in several key areas. In this section you will learn how to develop a Communication Strategy that conveys this kind of message.

Let's think about AdCom's focus on the future for a minute. If AdCom is focused on the future, they are not going to admit you solely on the strength of your many admirable qualities, or your impressive past accomplishments. Many failed applicants think that AdCom bestows acceptance letters as rewards for intelligence or past achievement. These applicants focus their applications entirely on "emphasizing their strengths and offsetting their weaknesses" and expect that their high GMAT score coupled with their numerous great stories about business successes, leadership and so on will be enough to earn them admission. They will often fail, because they have a mistaken understanding of what AdCom is looking for and consequently they've provided the wrong information.

However, it's important not to take AdCom's focus on the future to an extreme. AdCom is not going to be impressed by ambitious stories about your future success with no evidence offered in support. Some applicants believe that AdCom gives out admissions as a charity towards applicants with great, unfulfilled dreams. Applicants who think AdCom works this way

> **AdCom is going to make a carefully calculated bet – a gamble – on your future contributions and successes.**

submit applications with great plans to, say, establish a high-tech startup that will change the world. But they neglect to provide credible evidence of having the engineering or science background that is obviously necessary to found such a start-up. Instead of receiving charity from AdCom, they will receive a rejection letter, because they, too, have misunderstood what AdCom is looking for and have used a flawed strategy to market themselves.

AdCom isn't necessarily going to reward you for what a great, accomplished person you are. They are also not going to give you charity just because you have some fantastic dream. AdCom is going to make a carefully calculated bet – a gamble – on your future contributions and successes. They're going to place their bets on the applicants they believe are most likely to attend the school if admitted, make the campus a richer place, succeed in the most spectacular way, and become prominent alumni who lend status to the school – and who will also hopefully donate a lot of money to the school.

AdCom members, with their focus on future contributions and career development, want to place bets on applicants who not only articulate exciting dreams of future success, but also concrete evidence that the applicant has most of the qualities needed to achieve those dreams – and that he or she has a plan to add the qualities they are missing, and that this plan includes coming to business school and contributing to the education and enjoyment of their classmates.

Perhaps your colleagues are impressed that you can complete a DCF model faster than anyone else in the office, that you stayed up all night to finish that presentation, or that you make the highest average sales per client call. But AdCom does not necessarily care about these as stand-alone achievements. In fact, they may not even immediately appreciate the significance of your most impressive accomplishments if you do not explain them in the right terms (recall the example above of "shaving basis points off the LIBOR spread"). They will care much more about an achievement if you can convincingly link it to your career development. For example, telling AdCom "I make DCF models faster than anyone else in the office, which has earned me strong performance reviews every year. So I am smart enough to have a great career in banking. Let me tell you about this really technically difficult DCF model I did for the largest ever palm oil refinery IPO in Indonesia..." merely paints you as a smart guy adept at "some quantitative tasks junior finance people do." That's good, but it doesn't really stand out. "I want to improve bank stability. The fact that I can make a DCF model faster than anyone else means I can earn rapid promotions early on, quickly landing me in executive positions where I can begin to use my quantitative skills to establish new risk management techniques. I'd also like to run workshops on DCF modeling for your school's Finance Club" makes you look like a rising star who knows how to ride technical competence along a developmental path to a greater goal, and who will also be conscientious about contributing to the school community.

The 3Cs

AdCom is looking for evidence that you are going to be a valuable addition to their program. Broadly speaking, they are going to evaluate you along the same three dimensions as any selective organization uses: Competence, Commitment, and Culture. Competence, simply put, is your ability to succeed. Commitment is a measure of your interest in the MBA program and your future career. Culture is your

fit with the espoused values of the school. In other words: Can you do it? Do you want it? Do we like you?

This is a very broad conceptual framework that should help you start thinking about how you need to appeal to AdCom. As discussed above, past accomplishments alone are not enough to get you into an MBA program. That's because they speak primarily to competence, but unless they are couched in the right kind of story and presentation – the right kind of communication strategy – they do not speak to commitment and culture. You may be a great financial modeler but unless you show that you're committed to the school and some long term goals, and that you fit with the school's culture, AdCom will not believe that in future you will attend their school, contribute to their community, and successfully pursue interesting career goals.

The 3Cs

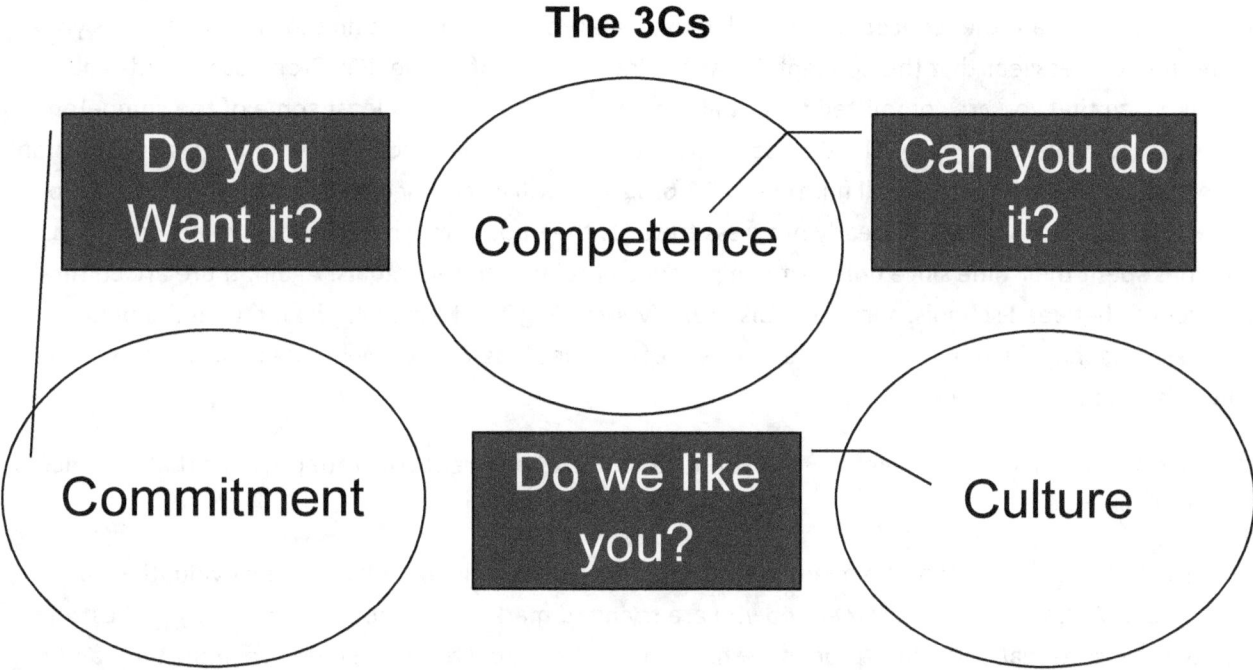

The 3Cs are good concepts to keep in mind, but they are a bit too broad to be useful in planning an application. Therefore, we should take a closer look at concrete qualities that exist within each of these dimensions. If we take competence, for example, it's probably true that some measure of intellectual power is highly related to your ability to achieve business goals. Similarly, within culture, your adherence to basic ethical guidelines is an important consideration for AdCom. And in terms of commitment, the amount of effort you show in preparing your application and learning about each school you apply to is going to be noticed by AdCom – remember, they want to be as sure as possible that you will attend if

you are accepted, and the effort you make to learn about the school is a strong indicator of your likeliness to attend.

However, to view the 3Cs as 3 independent dimensions is inaccurate and misleading. In fact, they overlap quite broadly. It's evident that many of the concepts discussed in Section 1 of this guide fit into more than one of the 3Cs. For example, the necessity of having a clear career goal fits into both commitment and culture. Goals are not really worth much if you are not committed to them, and they are also not going to impress an MBA AdCom if they do not fit into the general MBA culture – which has an emphasis on organizational leadership and career development. Indeed, different schools have cultures that are more welcoming to different kinds of goals; for example, some MBA programs are culturally more entrepreneurial than others, and others have a cultural preference for leadership of existing large organizations.

If we think about another concept discussed above, the progress you have already made towards your goals, it becomes clear that this concept lies at the intersection of all the 3Cs. Progress towards your goal is a sign that you are committed to it. It also shows that you have at least some of the competencies necessary to achieve it. Finally, the degree of progress you have made towards your goal is an important aspect of cultural fit – virtually all full-time MBA programs will discourage mid-career executives who have accumulated 20 years of steady progress towards their goals; much as they will reject someone who has spent their time since university on pursuits unrelated to their goals. Again, there are cultural differences between schools: some schools prefer very young applicants who haven't yet made much progress but show high potential, while others prefer their students to have made a bit more progress towards their goal before studying.

Below is a chart that shows how the 3Cs overlap, and the 15 different concrete qualities that exist across the 3C universe.

This is a conceptual model of the qualities AdCom officers are likely to look for when evaluating you. Remember, AdCom is your customer and you are trying to market yourself to it. AdCom, your customer, wants to be sure that you—the "product"—have most of the qualities it believes are important, and have the potential to develop whichever ones are missing, before "buying." If you can make a convincing marketing message along these lines, you are far along the way to making AdCom want to "buy" your application.

Overlapping Dimensions of the 3Cs

Intellect

Communication

Competence

Management

Maturity

Teamwork

Domain Skills

Leadership

Progress

Uniqueness

Commitment

Culture

Effort

Involvement

Ethics

Determination

Goals

Innovation

To a certain extent, the ingredients for your future success will be defined by your career goals. If you want to reform the banking sector, you need to understand finance. If you want to set up a national chain of dance studios, you need to have a talent for dance. But to a large degree, a given AdCom member is going to look for a very similar set of qualities in all applicants. This is because AdCom believes that no matter what your career path, in order to finally succeed, you are eventually going to be challenged in many of the same ways. Both the dance studio owner and the bank CEO are going to have to master communication and leadership skills that help them interact with clients and lead subordinates; they will both need a strong enough ethical backbone to keep them out of scandals; they are both going to need management skills to ensure their business runs smoothly, and so on.

It is important to note that, like many other concepts in this guide, the 3Cs model is a simplified generalization of a much more varied and complex reality. It is certainly not the case that every AdCom member at every MBA program has a 3Cs model that they refer to as they review applications. In fact, the chances are slim that any given AdCom member has even heard of this model. As described earlier

in this guide, the exact mix of qualities any given AdCom member is looking for is going to be different from the qualities any other given AdCom member wants, even if they both serve at the same school. The 3C conceptual model is intended to be broad enough that it contains at least some qualities that appeal strongly to all (or at least, most) AdCom members.

Ideally, you would know exactly which AdCom member would be evaluating your application, and you would be able to sit down with him prior to applying and learn exactly how he planned to evaluate you, so that you could write an application perfectly tailored to his preferences. But unfortunately, this ideal situation is impossible. Because you cannot tailor your application for the specific individual who will read it, applying a model that gets most things right most of the time is the next best solution.

If you were to ask any individual AdCom member what he looks for in an applicant, he would probably provide a list that did not upon an initial glance have much similarity to the 3Cs model in its terminology and organization. However, if you analyzed what his list was trying to measure, you would probably find that the 3Cs model did a pretty good job of capturing most of what he was looking for. Hence, the value of the 3Cs model is not that it can perfectly address the needs of any individual AdCom member. Rather, the value is that it is a single model that can address the needs of most AdCom members pretty well.

> *Because you cannot tailor your application for the specific individual who will read it, applying a model that gets most things right most of the time is the next best solution.*

It's important to note here that the 15 qualities defined within the 3Cs model can be interpreted differently by different schools, or even by different members of the same AdCom. In the definitions below, some of the more obvious differences in interpretation are mentioned. For simplicity, the text states that these differences in interpretation exist between schools, though in reality individual AdCom members can hold interpretations that contrast with what is normal at their own schools.

So as you learn and apply the 3Cs model, keep the following common-sense suggestions in mind:

- The 3Cs model is simple enough to be flexible. Take advantage of this flexibility if the situation calls for it. For example, if you learn that a particular school includes qualities not in the 3Cs model, excludes some qualities that are in the model, or has a slightly different definition of a quality, simply adjust the 3Cs model to suit the reality of that particular school.

- Don't refer to the 3Cs model in your application or during an interview. For example, telling an interviewer "I think I demonstrated the 'domain skills quality' in the XYZ project" is going to confuse her.

The qualities within the 3Cs model are discussed below in detail.

Competence

Life is not a Disney movie: sometimes no matter how much you want something, and no matter how hard to try, you simply are not talented enough to get it. This is where competence comes in. Competence measures whether you have the abilities – raw talent combined with learned skills and knowledge – to successfully complete your MBA degree, and go on to have a fruitful career. There are two qualities that are entirely located within competence: *intellect* and *communication.*

- **Intellect:** Your native intelligence, and ability to think clearly, perform computations, analysis and synthesis, and learn quickly. AdCom is aware that there is at best a weak correlation between intellectual horsepower and business success. And your ultimate career goal may not require high levels of intellectual or analytical ability. However, MBA courses require strong intellectual capacity to complete, and most recent MBA graduates find themselves in intellectually and analytically challenging roles. Thus, you are unlikely to ever get a chance to achieve your goals if you don't have strong intellectual capabilities to make it through first your MBA and then your first few years of post-MBA employment. GMAT scores and undergraduate transcripts (as well as the overall academic reputation of your undergraduate school) are the primary indicators of intellect, and evaluating these is fairly straightforward for AdCom. Intellectually demanding pre-MBA jobs are also a good indicator of intellect.

> *AdCom is aware that there is at best a weak correlation between intellectual horsepower and business success.*

- **Communication:** Your ability to communicate clearly, succinctly and effectively across generational, cultural and linguistic divides. Both at business school and afterwards, you need to be able to structure your communications in such a way that they make sense and are convincing – otherwise, you are going to have a lot of trouble working with other people. You also need to be able to take your audience's cultural background into consideration to maximize

> *Being able to communicate in multiple languages and across multiple cultures will go far in strengthening your application, but English proficiency is a pre-requisite for acceptance to virtually every major MBA program in the world.*

communication effectiveness. Being able to communicate in multiple languages and across multiple cultures will go far in strengthening your application, but English proficiency is a pre-requisite for acceptance at virtually every major MBA program in the world. The group discussion-oriented nature of MBA programs means that you need to be highly proficient in oral English before you start; MBA programs have the strictest oral English fluency requirements of any degree program. If you are a non-native English speaker, AdCom will want to ensure you can communicate effectively in English because English is the international language of business and the only language used at most top business schools. AdCom will look at the clarity of your essays and your performance in interviews to get a sense of your native communication ability. If you grew up in a non-English environment, they will also consider your TOEFL or IELTS score. AdCom will look for evidence of cross-cultural communication competence in your academic, work, or personal experiences.

Culture

Sometimes you just fit in with a group right away, and other times you have trouble getting along with them. These outcomes are largely due to individual and organizational cultures. In our definition, culture is a measure of your values, personality, way of looking at the world, and way of interacting with others. The Cultural compatibility of an individual with an organization is often referred to as *fit*. From your job-hunting experiences, you may have heard phrases like "I was given a *fit* interview" or "this person does not have a lot of *fit* with our company." These are comments about culture. There are two qualities of culture: *innovation* and *ethics*.

- *Innovation:* Your ability to invent, expand, develop – or at least adopt and adapt to – new ideas, methodologies, and concepts in the real world; and your ability to use a mix of common sense and imagination to resolve seemingly intractable problems. The business world is fast-moving – new technologies come and go, regional trade patterns evolve over time, and business models must constantly be redesigned. If you are to succeed, you will need to be at or near the forefront of innovation, and to have the flexibility to quickly solve new, unexpected challenges. Keep in mind that different schools and AdCom members are looking for different levels of innovation in their applicants. While probably no one wants students who lack innovation, some schools look for more innovative people while others place less emphasis on this quality. To judge innovation, AdCom will look for evidence that you have thought outside of the box, have participated in developing new ideas, products or strategies, and have found new ways to look at and resolve problems that others could not solve.

- **Ethics:** At its simplest, ethics refers to your trustworthiness, honesty, and moral character. As you struggle up the ladder of success you will often face temptations to either cheat to hasten your climb, or unfairly take advantage of your increasing power and influence. Falling for these temptations can not only ruin your career, but can also reflect poorly on your MBA alma mater. AdCom wants to see evidence that you maintained high ethical standards not just in everyday life, but in exceptional situations where no one was looking and the potential benefits of unethical behavior were high. Many AdComs will ask you to demonstrate your ethical values by asking you to discuss a "moral dilemma," in which you chose between two valid, but conflicting, ethical standards and there was no clear right answer. For example, you gain confidential information that a trusted colleague who is about to buy a new house is going to be laid off by your company. Do you choose to tell your friend and betray your company or keep the secret and betray your friend? Either choice is valid as long as you can explain your ethical basis for it. Note that after major economic crashes (in which many corporate scandals usually come to light), MBA programs in general tend to place more weight on ethics.

> *If you are great in every objective measure but appear cocky, Berkeley may decide you do not share their ethical values and reject you.*

There is also a more complex aspect to the ethics quality. Many schools seek students who embody specific values; these values are not objectively right or wrong, but rather they are subjective worldviews or personality traits. A very good example is Berkeley Haas, which places a great emphasis on creating "collaborative leaders who possess confidence without attitude." If you are great in every objective measure but appear cocky, Berkeley may decide you do not share their ethical values and reject you.

Commitment

As Albert Einstein famously said, success is 1% inspiration and 99% perspiration. Professional success does not come easily. If you are not committed to pursuing your career goals, even in the face of failures and difficulties, you are not likely to achieve them. Moreover, the competition for admission to MBA programs keeps getting fiercer, and with AdComs strongly incentivized to only accept students who will definitely matriculate, showing that you are committed to each school you apply to is important to your application.

- *Determination:* Your ability to pursue goals in the face of great challenges, temporary failures, and uncertainty, and generally persevere in the face of defeat or difficulty. AdCom will want to see evidence that you have ignored temptations, made sacrifices, displayed self-discipline, and overcome crises and obstacles in your pursuit of goals. If you have not, they will fear that you are not mentally and emotionally tough enough to overcome the obstacles you will certainly face in the future. Perhaps you have not yet had a chance to display exceptional determination in pursuing your career goals, but AdCom will be impressed by determination displayed in the pursuit of any other goal.

- *Effort:* The effort you have evidently put into learning about the school and putting together a good application package. To reiterate a point already made several times in this guide: schools only want to offer admissions to students they think are likely to matriculate. Because they can't read your mind, AdCom members will judge your likeliness to accept an offer in large part by the effort you put into the

> *Schools want to see that you made an extra effort to learn about them by talking to alumni, attending recruiting seminars or visiting campus.*

application. Part of effort involves simple things like making sure your essays are proofread and nicely formatted. But it goes far beyond this. Most schools will expect you to write an essay describing how you see their MBA serving your career goals. The more specific and insightful you can be about the school, the more impressed they will be. You can do some online research to learn basic facts you can write into these essays. But schools want to see more – they want to see that you made an extra effort to learn about them by talking to alumni, attending recruiting seminars, or visiting campus. In fact, some schools now require applicants to answer essay questions about the efforts they have taken to learn about the school prior to applying (for example: NYU Stern). Towards the end of any MBA interview you participate in, your interviewer will almost always allow you to ask questions about the program. Do not mistake this for a polite nicety. The interviewer is trying to judge the effort you've put into learning about his school by testing the sophistication of the questions you are able to ask. If you ask questions whose answers can be found on the school's website, you are not going to earn points for effort.

Competence and culture

Sometimes personal competence is not enough. A business leader must be able to engage other individuals to achieve her objectives. To do so, she must have cultural traits that allow her to motivate,

lead, and cooperate with others. Thus, at the intersection of competence and culture, we find two important interpersonal, or soft, skills: *leadership* and *teamwork*.

- **Leadership:** Your ability to motivate others, bring teams together, nurture talent, and impact or change organizations. There are two misconceptions that many applicants have about leadership. The first is to confuse leadership with management. Leadership is not the same as management, and confusing the two qualities can weaken your application considerably. Leadership is about motivating other people to do something they would not otherwise do. In contrast, management is about improving the performance of some task that's happening already. The second misconception is that leadership can only be demonstrated in formal team-leader positions at work. In fact, leadership is most impressive when you exhibit it while you are *not* in an official supervisory role, and therefore lack formal authority, or when you bring together disparate groups with conflicting interests. Simply "leading" a project at work often does not actually demonstrate much leadership talent – you have formal authority, your team members have to obey your orders, and everyone usually starts off with the overriding shared interest of completing the project. These team-leader roles are usually better tests of your management ability than of your leadership ability. Schools may be more impressed with your leadership if you do something like convincing skilled colleagues to voluntarily participate in an informal training program you develop for new hires or interns.

> **Leadership is most impressive when you exhibit it while you are not in an official supervisory role.**

It is also important to note that, despite the definition above, there is a very strong cultural aspect to what is meant by the term leadership. Some schools equate leadership more with using superior presentation of ideas and force of personality to establish yourself as the leader and influence others to follow you (for example, Harvard). Other schools take a much different perspective, where leadership is seen more as creating and serving on teams, and in nurturing and mentoring colleagues and subordinates (for example, MIT Sloan). Make sure you understand each school's cultural perspective on leadership before applying.

However it is defined, leadership is one of the gold standards of MBA programs, because they like to view and advertise themselves as "creating business leaders." Therefore, AdCom will often ask you to describe leadership experiences in one of your application essays.

- **Teamwork:** Your ability to function constructively in different roles on a team, and also your ability to build friendly *relationships* with people from different cultures and backgrounds. Serving as a member of a cross-disciplinary, and quite possibly, multi-cultural and multi-lingual,

team will be one of the primary work environments you find yourself in during your entire career, so learning how to work with others is clearly going to be necessary for success. Even when you are in a distinct leadership role, understanding team dynamics gives you a large advantage in managing your subordinates. (And, as described above, some schools view leadership and teamwork as different aspects of the same indivisible meta-skill.) Building relationships with diverse groups of people – i.e., being extroverted and likeable – allows you to prosper in a global business world. AdCom will give you high scores for cooperation if you can show you worked in diverse (e.g., cross-disciplinary, international, etc.) groups and have demonstrated a willingness to make personal sacrifices (e.g., staying late to help another group member without gaining any recognition) to ensure group successes.

> *Some schools view leadership and teamwork as different aspects of the same indivisible meta-skill.*

Culture and commitment

Commitment is great, but it's not helpful if we are committed to the wrong values. And values that we profess but do not act on are worthless. At the nexus of culture and commitment are the activities that we participate in and the objectives that we set for ourselves. In this intersection, we find two qualities: *goals* and *involvement*.

- *Goals:* Your plan to succeed in the future, not just by "doing well," but by building or achieving something concrete and lasting. You gain a lot of credibility for having solid goals if you can demonstrate commitment: i.e., that you have already been pursuing them for a number of years, and if you evoke obvious passion about them. You must show that your goals have a clear relationship to the MBA you want to pursue. AdCom will look for meaningful, clear and logical future plans – effectively, the content of your Mission Statement.

- *Involvement:* Your engagement with your community, beyond the formal requirements and responsibilities of your job. Such engagement can range from devoted, long term involvement with a non-profit or NGO, to simply joining the office social committee to organize social events for your colleagues. Generally speaking, an activity only counts towards involvement if you are not compensated for it (with important exceptions; most notably, if your full-time job is with an NGO, you will get high marks for involvement even though you are undoubtedly receiving compensation for your work, albeit probably on a below-market pay scale).

While involvement is arguably not directly related to future business success, AdCom members usually want to admit students who will play an active role on campus and share their

56

knowledge and talents with their classmates – after all, MBA campuses have strongly student-driven cultures. Moreover, especially when applying to North American programs, showing you have been committed to an active role in your community says a lot to AdCom about your well-roundedness and socialization, and also your ethical values. Involvement can be demonstrated by volunteer activities you have performed during and after your undergraduate years. Note that long term activities that include a planning or leadership role are much more impressive than occasional participation in seemingly random volunteer events.

As a matter of course, many would-be MBA applicants, especially in America, make sure to participate in some form of community service during college and/or while working. This type of service can include a very wide range of activities, from tutoring disadvantaged children to working in an advocacy group to organizing a local basketball league to helping a large NGO

> *Many would-be MBA applicants, especially in America, make sure to participate in some form of community service during college and/or while working.*

with its fundraising strategy. The applicants make sure to mention this service on their resume and quite possibly use a story from their community service experiences in one of their essays.

Ideally, you will have already been active in some form of community service prior to this point. If not, you have a few choices about what you want to do:

o   Get involved in some form of community service now. Presumably you are reading this guide several months before your applications are due, so you will have time to amass at least some significant experience. However, beware of making it seem obvious that you have pursued community service for the sole purpose of writing about it on your MBA application!

o   Think about something you have done in the past that can be recast as a form of community service. Even things like helping to run a student social organization during college, tutoring a classmate in one or two subjects, or mentoring some of your junior employees at work can be portrayed as forms of community service. Think about roles you have taken on within any community you belong to, for which you did not receive financial compensation. Some activities you did not originally consider to be community service probably qualify. We have worked with many clients who have told us something like "I don't have time for community service because I have so many obligations to run Sunday school and summer camps for my church!"

- o Recognize that you have not made significant contributions in this area and try to make up for it by thinking about ways you want to contribute to your campus community once at business school. This strategy may expose you to charges of not being sufficiently involved in your community in the past, but can be superior to unconvincing attempts at the first two suggestions above.

Commitment and competence

Raw ability is not enough, and neither is unguided enthusiasm. Talent and hard work directed over time towards achieving a goal may not guarantee success, but they certainly increase its likelihood. At the intersection of commitment and competence, there are two qualities that show an ability to channel talent and enthusiasm towards incrementally accomplishing tasks and pursuing goals over time: management and domain skills.

- *Management:* Your ability to make short and long term plans and execute them, delegate and evaluate work, and supervise processes. Management is hard, because it requires competencies in organization that do not come naturally to most of us, and because these competencies only yield rewards if they are consistently applied over time, which means that a certain amount of zeal and discipline is required to manage successfully. It is very important to understand that while it is common in the business press to conflate management with leadership, in real life and in the eyes of AdCom, management is complementary to, but distinct from, leadership. Management is ultimately about planning, supervising and modifying processes with an eye to efficiency, whereas leadership has little if anything to do with processes or efficiency. It is very common for a person to be a strong manager but weak leader or vice versa, so evidence of one quality is not necessarily evidence of the other. To judge your management ability, AdCom will look for work experiences in which you were in any kind of formal planning, management or supervisory role, and in which you were effective at setting and reaching targets.

> **Management is complementary to, but distinct from, leadership.**

- *Domain Skills:* Skills and knowledge that are specific to your planned career. For example, someone who wants to go into finance probably needs strong financial modeling skills and an understanding of markets, while someone who wants to build a tech startup probably needs an engineering education. Domain skills are special competencies that you build up over a period of years in order to better pursue goals you are committed to. They are generally easy to demonstrate from your resume and past work experience, and AdCom will start looking here. Career switchers will receive particularly close scrutiny of their domain skill quality. If you lack the domain skills and knowledge of your proposed new career, you will need a very clear explanation of how you will gain them during or after your MBA.

Competence, culture and commitment

Sometimes it takes the right mix of skills, character and enthusiasm to be successful. Where all of the 3Cs intersect, we find three important qualities: *maturity, uniqueness* and *progress.*

- *Maturity:* Your willingness to take criticism, acknowledge weaknesses, and learn from failures, as well as your self-knowledge of your own personal values and motivations. Everyone is going to fail a few times on the road to success, and AdCom wants to be sure you are the type who will see failures as a chance for learning and self-improvement, rather than either lose your composure or pretend the failure never happened. AdCom will look for examples where you kept composure during, and learned from, public failure, and will expect you to acknowledge your weaknesses. Many schools prompt applicants to address this topic by requiring essays about failure. Even if you are not prompted to talk about maturity, try to sprinkle examples of failures you've overcome and difficult decisions you've made in your essays. Note that the worst thing you can do when presented with a question that addresses your maturity is to try and dodge the question with a foolish, non-introspective answer like "my biggest weakness is that I work too hard," or "my biggest failure was not insisting that I only work with people who are as smart as I am." AdCom also wants to see that you understand your own values and motivations and how they link to your career goals. Many aspects of the self-knowledge required to show maturity should be explicit in the Mission Statement you developed in Section 1.

- *Progress:* Your progress towards your career goals, measured relative to the resources and time you have used to make that progress. Progress is a reasonable measure of commitment and competence. It is also strongly related to the can-do cultural ethos of business schools – if you are unable to find constructive ways to use your time and abilities without business school, AdCom members are unlikely to want to take a risk on you. Also, different schools have a preference for students at different points in their careers: some prefer bright young hotshots barely out of college, and others prefer students with several years of work experience under their belts.

It is sometimes not evident to AdCom exactly how much progress a certain achievement represents. For example, if you are promoted to Vice President of a small or unknown company, AdCom simply doesn't know if this is a significant

> *An American AdCom officer knows how to evaluate progress made in small American firms or famous international firms; he does not know how to evaluate progress made in unfamiliar foreign firms.*

achievement or not, and is likely to discount it. In contrast, even working at an entry level position in a prestigious multinational company will often get you credit for making progress. This is because AdCom has a high degree of certainty of what criteria you had to meet to get the job, and what kind of work you did on a daily basis. This tendency to ascribe more value to progress made in well-known companies explains why most accepted foreign applicants to world-leading MBA programs come from the overseas offices of elite American and European firms, not from foreign companies. An American AdCom officer knows how to evaluate progress made in small American firms or famous international firms; he does not know how to evaluate progress made in unfamiliar foreign firms.

American schools especially are known for making efforts to measure the progress of applicants against the socioeconomic resources they have been able to call upon. This interest in leveling the playing field to help applicants from disadvantaged backgrounds lies behind application questions like "what ethnicity are you?" (In the U.S., ethnicity is often used as a proxy for socio-economic status.) "Are you the first person in your family to attend college?" And "What are the professions of your parents?"

While MBA programs are generally less concerned about leveling the playing field than most other academic departments – after all, a strong family background is an advantage in business that can make your career goals more credible – they are still likely to measure your accomplishments against what resources you've used to reach them. Therefore, you should be careful about bragging about how high status and wealthy your family is on your application; doing so will usually raise AdCom's expectations of how much progress you should have made so far in life. Never let pride or shame lead you to exaggerate your socioeconomic background on your application forms!

- *Uniqueness:* How you are different from other applicants – whether in terms of ethnicity, gender, life experience, commitments, talents, etc. Top schools, especially in the U.S., place a high value on having diverse classes, and take steps to admit genuinely unique applicants over "standard" candidates. Note that some aspects of uniqueness can be entirely unrelated to your career goals – uniqueness is perceived by many AdCom members to have intrinsic value. However, if you have some unique knowledge or skills that are relevant to business, and are either something you can share with your classmates or leverage to achieve your career goals, that is even more valuable.

Uniqueness is great up to a point, but being too unique can make you seem like a misfit – this is one quality where achieving balance is critical.

> **Uniqueness is great up to a point, but being too unique can make you seem like a misfit.**

60

A white male applicant who went to an Ivy League school and then worked for a big investment bank should devote considerable time to figuring out and explaining what makes him distinct from all the other applicants with identical backgrounds. Even an irrelevant skill, like the ability to juggle 5 burning torches at the same time is better than nothing at all. On the other hand, someone who went to Divinity School and then went to work for an anti-big-business environmental group is probably so unique that she looks "different" (with a negative connotation), and she will need to focus on explaining how she can ever fit into business school.

Self-Diagnosis Along the 3Cs

Now that you have identified what qualities AdCom wants to see in you, and you understand what these qualities mean to AdCom and what kind of evidence AdCom will look for to evaluate you, it is time to diagnose yourself along each quality. As in the past chapter, brutal objectivity and honesty is critical to this self-diagnosis. You are only setting yourself up for failure if you refuse to admit that you are stronger along some qualities than others.

Indeed, objectivity and an evidence-led approach are the keys to this exercise. Though you are diagnosing yourself, you are diagnosing yourself based on objective evidence that you can provide AdCom. Imagine you are trying to make a case in front of a court of law. The law, you would learn if you were to ask a judge, is concerned not with what is actually true, but rather with what can be demonstrated with evidence. If you were a defendant in a murder case, and your alibi was that on the

> **AdCom can only judge you based on the evidence you are able to provide.**

night of the murder you were home alone watching TV, you would be in trouble. Your alibi would be *true*, but because you were alone, there would be no witnesses to provide evidence to support it. Therefore, if you were diagnosing your legal case, you would have to give yourself a very low score for your alibi.

The need for evidence is equally necessary in this exercise, because AdCom can only judge you based on the evidence you are able to provide. So while you may be the smartest math whiz you've ever met, if you had a bad day when you took the GMAT and your score does not reflect your math ability, you will have to rank yourself as weak or average in terms of intellect unless you can think of some other evidence to offset your GMAT score. On the flip side of the equation, the focus on evidence can be to your advantage: if you are terrible at math but managed to guess your way through the GMAT quantitative section and achieve a score in the 95th percentile – well, as far as anyone looking at the evidence is concerned, you have a lot of intellectual horsepower, so give yourself a high score here.

For another example of how to use evidence to your advantage, assume you have recently decided that your goal is to open up a chain of dance studios. This is actually a new idea – until 6 months ago you had

always wanted to pursue a career in finance and you were, in fact, working at an investment bank. So you know that in reality your passion about setting up a dance studio is open to question. However, you took dance classes as a child and during your previous career in finance you worked on some projects for companies with chain stores. Bingo. You can score yourself mid-to-high on goals because you can point to objective evidence that you've been involved in dancing your whole life (if, by chance, you only attended that dance class as a child because your parents made you, it doesn't matter because AdCom doesn't know), and during your stint in finance – a job you can convincingly claim you took to gain exposure to the financing methods and business strategies your chain will need as it grows – you ensured you worked on projects for companies with the kind of franchise model you want to adopt.

It is important to understand that the "quality" of your evidence is usually more important than the "quantity" of your evidence. That is to say, AdCom cares about how you used the quality in question more than they care about how much money or staff were involved. For example, AdCom will not necessarily be more impressed with Applicant 1 if his evidence for some quality involves a $500 million deal, while Applicant 2's evidence only involves a $50 thousand deal. However, AdCom will definitely be more impressed with Applicant 2 if she convinces them that on her $50 thousand deal she really demonstrated and developed this quality, while Applicant 1 appears to have completed his $500 million deal in spite of being weaker in the same quality.

Wherever you are relatively weak – perhaps you are simply bad at math and analysis, so your score for intellect is low, or perhaps you've been working in public relations and lack basic domain skills you need for your career goal in product management – consider concrete steps you can take to improve yourself. Often, you can ask for new assignments at work, take outside coursework at a local college, or get involved in a volunteer program outside of work. For example, a person who is bad at math and analysis could ask for assignments at work that will challenge his math skills, or take an algebra course. The public relations officer could ask to temporarily switch to the marketing department and enroll in accounting classes. Someone weak in communication could volunteer to help an NGO with its international fundraising efforts. Taking these concrete steps gives 2 important signals to AdCom. 1: You are serious about improving this weakness. 2: By the time you start school, you probably will be stronger than you are now.

> *AdCom cares about how you used the quality more than they care about how much money or staff were involved.*

What is the basis against which you can measure yourself for the purpose of assigning your scores? Ideally, you can score yourself against people you know who are current students at, or recent alumni of, the kinds of schools you want to attend. Thus, you are scoring yourself relative to people who are a good proxy for your future classmates. If you don't know enough current or recent students to use them

as a basis for your self-diagnosis, try to use as a model other individuals in their late 20s and early 30s whom you admire for their business success.

Creating Your Admission Case

While working through your Communication Strategy you have thought in detail about what qualities your customer, AdCom, wants in applicants. Then you went through a self-diagnosis to evaluate your ability to demonstrate that you have each of these qualities. You've even thought about what preconceptions AdCom may have about you, and how you can encourage positive preconceptions and offset negative ones.

Now you are ready to put together your complete marketing message, or your *Admission Case*. This is a brief document – no more than a page in length – summarizing why you think AdCom should accept you. If you are familiar with the concept of the *elevator pitch*, you're now writing your elevator pitch. (An *elevator pitch* is the very brief spoken explanation that entrepreneurs prepare to summarize their business model and why it is worth investing in. The idea is to be prepared for the eventuality that they are ever in the same elevator as a potential investor, or are in some other situation where they have only a few moments to market their company to someone important.) In sum, your Admission Case is a self-contained, coherent and convincing argument for your admission.

At the heart of this message will be your original Mission Statement. Your Mission Statement is fundamental to any marketing pitch, not only because AdCom members are looking for applicants with a clear sense of mission, but because your Mission Statement forms a useful framework around which you can fill out the body of your Admission Case.

The bulk of your Admission Case should explain the evidence in support of your abilities along the 3Cs framework, and include any steps you are taking to improve yourself along any of the qualities (these steps probably include going to business school).

You should try to weave this Admission Case into a single narrative as much as possible. A narrative structure provides its own internal logic and is easy for a reader to follow. The closer you can get your Admission Case to a narrative form, the more convincing and self-contained an argument it is, and the easier it will be to convey orally to interviewers, recommendation letter writers, and other audiences. But don't worry too much about making it pretty – your Admission Case can be full of grammar errors and notes to yourself because AdCom will never see it. The sample Admission Case below includes notes about which of the 15 qualities each aspect of the case is relevant to.

Self-Diagnosis Using the *AKAD Excel Worksheet*

It is easy enough to diagnose yourself with a pen and paper, but the ***AKAD Excel Worksheet*** has a tab called "Communication Strat Worksheet" that facilitates this self-diagnosis process, and will even provide you with a graphical summary of your profile. In each sub-category, score yourself a 1 to 5, with 1 being "weak" and 5 being "strong." Note that you can only enter whole numbers, not fractions. The point of this exercise is to perform a general self-diagnosis to help guide your Communication Strategy, not to waste time worrying whether your experience leading the college dance committee merits a 3.4 or 3.5 in the leadership quality. If sticking to integers from 1 to 5 still seems unsatisfying, consider that this method gives you 5^{15}, or over 30 billion, possible combinations of scores.

To ensure that you are maintaining an evidence-based approach, right next to each score, write down the reasoning for your score and the evidence you use to support your reasoning. Keep yourself honest: evidence must be something that will be convincing to others – "Mom always told me I'm creative" is not evidence that you score high on innovation. "Independently developed new approach to online marketing during the ABC project" probably is. The more convincing evidence you have, the higher your score should be. In qualities where you have a score of 3 or lower, you should also record what you could do prior to your application or matriculation to improve your score.

The ***AKAD Excel Worksheet*** will show you what typical applicant category you most closely fit, and provide some insight into what preconceptions AdCom may form about you based on that category, and how to profit from positive preconceptions and offset negative ones. While this is a useful and interesting tool, treat its output as a collection of ideas to take under consideration, not as a verdict on the kind of impression AdCom members are fated to have of you.

Sample Admission Case

Since I was a teenager and saw the economic dislocation caused by the 199x recession, I have always wanted to help reform my country's banking sector to prevent future financial crises (Goals). I worked my way through college to get a finance degree (Determination) and got a 3.75 GPA (Intellect.) I founded a number of finance-related clubs and invested lots of time in growing them into lasting institutions (Leadership, Management, Involvement – note that these are weak examples of leadership and management and I will need to come up with better evidence.)

After graduation I took a job in a commercial bank to pursue this objective (Goals). There, I realized that while I am good at quantitative analysis, as demonstrated by my financial modeling ability (Domain Skills), I needed to develop many other skills. This was demonstrated clearly by my failure in the XYZ project, in which I focused too much on the quant analysis but failed to understand the client's preconceptions, and thereby my suggestions were not accepted (Communication – need to improve!) My reaction was to take the blame and apologize (Ethics), leverage advice from colleagues who better understood the client (Teamwork), and come back with a more appropriate proposal (Maturity, Determination).

I have demonstrated other qualities necessary for success. I have excellent problem-solving abilities as demonstrated by my improvement of BIG Corporation's M&A strategy to reduce costs while retaining all synergies (Innovation). I was also quick to re-design XYZ's fundraising strategy to recognize the reality that raising high amounts of debt during the current financial crisis would not be possible (Innovation, Domain Skills.)

I have done pretty well so far, as demonstrated by my recent promotion (Progress), but to proceed in my career, I need a broader education in business strategy and other business topics (Maturity, Domain Skills – need to improve via B-school). I will do this first by going to business school. I have noted that the following courses and programs at your school would be especially beneficial for me in the following ways … (Effort.) After graduating, I would like to work for a management consultancy. From there I can jump back into the commercial banking world at a much more senior level (Goals).

While I am at school, I think I can add a lot to the campus. I want to participate in the finance club (Involvement, Goals), and I also want to run a school play, as I have been active in theatre for my whole life and note that your school has an annual theater review (Uniqueness, Involvement, Effort).

You will eventually divide up your Admission Case into pieces that you distribute across your application. For example, one part of your Admission Case will be addressed in essay 1, while a second part is primarily covered in your resume, and a third part will rely on a recommendation letter. The logistics of

how to assign your Admission Case to different parts of your application is covered in the next section: Application Preparation.

Section 3: Application Preparation

As you plan your application, there are two main issues you need to keep in mind:

- Your application should be a self-contained, coherent and convincing argument for your admission. That means, your application should express your Admission Case.

- Your application, as much as possible, should touch on as many of the qualities within the 3Cs model as possible, to be appealing to as broad an audience of AdCom members as possible.

Mapping Your Application to the 3Cs

The first step, therefore, in preparing your application should be to map out which part of your Admission Case, and which of the 15 qualities in the 3Cs model, each part of your application will address.

Simply put, there are 5 major parts of your application:

- Scores: GMAT, TOEFL, transcripts (GPA);

- Resume: The summary of your education and work experience; for our purposes we also include application forms into this category because they usually comprise a more comprehensive form of your resume;

- Essays: The personal statements you provide to the school;

- Recs: The recommendation letters that you provide in support of your candidacy;

- Interview: Your face-to-face interaction with an AdCom member or alumnus.

It's important to note that in most cases interviews are by invitation only (there are notable exceptions, like Kellogg, but even Kellogg has started to back away from its longstanding universal interview policy). This means you only get an interview if the first 4 parts – your *written application* – are good enough to justify one. So you need to cover as much of your Admission Case as possible in these 4 written submissions.

Let's look broadly at how a typical applicant could map the different parts of their application across the 3Cs. Keep in mind, however, that because every applicant is different, the exact mapping will vary from applicant to applicant.

Mapping Application to the 3Cs

	Scores	Resume	Essays	Recs	Interview
Competence	●	●	◖	◔	◖
Culture	○	◔	●	◖	●
Commitment	◔	◖	●	◖	●

Less relevant ○ ◀━━━▶ ● Very relevant

Scores: Your scores primarily indicate your intellect, which is part of competence. If you took the TOEFL, your TOEFL score will also contribute to AdCom's evaluation of your communication ability. To a certain extent, your scores can also suggest a level of determination. Yes, after all the time you put into studying for the GMAT and TOEFL, AdCom is only going to refer to your score to evaluate you along a narrow range of qualities.

Resume: Your resume can indicate a wide range of abilities. It is obviously a very clear indicator of your progress to date, but may also contain information relevant to intellect, management, leadership, involvement, uniqueness, domain skills, etc. AdCom may look at your resume as a general indicator about a broad range of qualities, though it will often look elsewhere for definitive proof.

Essays: Your essays are clearly the most important part of your written application in terms of providing AdCom insight into your culture and commitment. If you do not create a strong positive impression about these areas in your essays, your application will probably quickly end up in the "Rejection" pile.

Recs: Because recommendations come from other people, AdCom will give them great weight in judging qualities that are hard to prove objectively. After all, a third party's advocacy of your teamwork and communication skills is often more convincing than your self-evaluation. Note, however, that recommendations appear on the chart above as being partially relevant to all dimensions. These scores reflect the flexibility of recommendations: if you use them wisely, they will reinforce you along whichever areas you look weakest.

AKAD Education Group

AKAD MBA Application Guide
www.akadgroup.com

Interview: In many ways, the interview serves the same function as the essays, as it primarily allows AdCom to judge your soft skills. However, while you can revise essays endlessly until they are perfect, you can't do so with an interview. Interviews give AdCom their chief information about how you appear and interact in real life.

Mapping Application to Qualities

	Scores	Resume	Essays	Recs	Interview
Intellect	●	◑	◑	◔	◔
Communicate	◑	◑	●	◑	●
Leadership	○	◑	●	◑	●
Teamwork	○	◑	●	◑	●
Ethics	○	◔	●	◑	●
Innovation	○	◑	●	◑	●
Goals	○	◔	●	◔	●
Involvement	○	◔	●	◑	●
Determination	◑	◔	●	◑	●
Effort	○	○	●	○	●
Management	○	◔	◔	◑	◑
Domain Skills	◔	●	◑	◑	◔
Maturity	○	○	●	◑	●
Progress	◑	●	◑	◑	◔
Uniqueness	○	◑	●	◑	●

Less relevant ○ ◁▮ ● Very relevant

69

Application mapping by qualities

Let's look at this application mapping from a different angle: which parts of the application will a typical applicant use to address each quality? (Again, keep in mind that this "typical" mapping is not going to hold true for every applicant applying to every school, and you should think about how you can adjust this mapping to suit your own needs.) For the time being, we'll leave the Recs column for a discussion later.

Intellect: For the most part, AdCom is going to look at your scores to indicate your raw intellectual capacity. You may also be able to suggest raw intellect on your resume – e.g., if you won some scholarships or had a particularly intellectually challenging job. Good, clear writing can be a sign of strong intellectual ability, as can stories about solving intellectual challenges.

Communication: Your ability to communicate clearly in written form will be very strongly demonstrated by your essays. If you write clearly, you will get high scores for communication. Your TOEFL score, if applicable, and (to a lesser degree) GMAT verbal score also provide insight into your communication ability. Your interviewer will also be judging how clearly you communicate during your discussion, and may also ask you to talk about communication-related experiences. Communication can also be demonstrated by experiences working with people from different backgrounds, which you can include on your resume or discuss in one or more essays.

Leadership: Your leadership is primarily going to be evident from the stories you tell in your essays – indeed, most schools will ask you to address your leadership abilities in at least one essay. Depending on your work and extra-curricular experience, your leadership may also be evident on your resume. While listing "Investment Bank Analyst" will not give you automatic credit for leadership, listing "Military Officer" might. Many interviewers will attempt to learn about your leadership experience, as this is one of the primary areas where they aim to judge you.

Teamwork: This quality will largely come through in your essays. Some schools will ask you to describe a team experience, which is an obvious place to address teamwork. If not, you can address teamwork in essay topics such as leadership or failure. Teamwork may be evident on your resume – especially if you have worked in roles that stress teamwork. Your interviewer will be judging how able you are to form constructive relationships (not necessarily by asking directly, but definitely by observing your behavior), and may also ask about teamwork experiences.

Ethics: Some schools will ask essay questions that require you to directly address your ethics (e.g., "Describe a moral dilemma you have faced"). If not, look for an opportunity to do so as part of your response to other essay questions (e.g., "What is most important to you and why?" or "How do you contribute to your community?"). Many interviewers will also ask about ethics, and recommendation letters frequently raise issues of ethics and integrity.

Innovation: Your innovativeness and problem-solving ability may be evident from your resume, especially if you have founded a company with a creative business model, or worked in R&D. Otherwise, you should seek to provide evidence of this quality in your essays – there are many ways to do so in essays that discuss leadership experiences, failures, and so on. Some schools even ask you to write an essay on something innovative you have done. You may also use an interview as an occasion to discuss your creativity (in some cases, you have to; Sloan almost always asks about creativity in its interviews).

Involvement: Involvement may be largely apparent from your resume – i.e., if you have had a substantial role in an NGO or student organization, you may list this information on your resume. Otherwise, you must seek to address this issue somewhere in your essays and interview, perhaps by writing or speaking about an experience that took place in the context of some kind of social involvement, or by talking about specific ways in which you would like to contribute to the campus community during your MBA.

Goals: Your essays are really the only venue in the written application for you to talk about your goals. Typically, there is at least one essay topic that asks you to address your career plan. Interviewers will also expect you to describe your goals clearly and succinctly, with a neat explanation of why your MBA is important to achieving them. Note that this is one of the few qualities where a recommendation letter is not going to help you. If you can't articulate your goals convincingly yourself, no one else's testimony is going to convince AdCom.

Determination: Usually, the best way of conveying your determination is in your essays. Many schools will ask you to answer essay topics such as "describe a failure" or "describe a time you were severely challenged." These topics are invitations for you to describe your determination in overcoming your failure or the challenges you faced. If there is no essay topic directly addressing determination, you should be sure to emphasize your tireless pursuit of your goals in one of the other essays. Determination will also sometimes come up in interviews. And you may be able to convey determination with your academic scores, if you can convincingly explain that you faced some special challenge during school (for example, you needed to work your way through college).

Effort: The amount of effort you put into your application is going to primarily shine through in your essays and interview. It is quite difficult to show effort anywhere else in your application. You can convey effort in your essays and interview by showing sophisticated knowledge about the school you're applying to, describing the efforts you have gone through to obtain this knowledge, and thoughtfully linking the school's characteristics with your own learning needs, interests and ability to contribute. In addition, submitting neatly prepared, well-edited essays is a strong sign of effort. An often fatal indicator of lack of effort is submitting essays that are obviously being reused in their entirety for multiple applications – such indifference becomes almost comically obvious when an applicant forgets to change the school name after copying an essay from one application to another.

Management: Management skills should be evident on your resume – if not from the nature of your jobs themselves, then through the specific accomplishments you list under your jobs or from clubs/activities you participated in at school. It is also relatively easy to refer to project management in one or more of your essays – e.g., in an essay on failure you could preface the failure itself by explaining you were managing a team of 5 people on a 3-month project. Interviews may or may not touch on management experience and ability.

Domain Skills: Your domain skills will most likely be evident from your resume. For example, if your career goal is to improve bank stability and your resume shows that you've studied finance and worked in a bank, you will get credit for possessing relevant domain skills. Depending on your field, domain skills may be evident from your transcript (in the scores section). You can easily find opportunities in your essays to display your pursuit and possession of domain skills. Interviewers might or might not ask detailed questions about this quality; the more in line your goals are with your past experience, the fewer questions they are likely to ask. Note that if you are a career switcher, AdCom may place special emphasis on this quality.

Maturity: Your understanding of your own strengths and weaknesses, ability to learn from failure, and other measures of maturity will come through almost entirely from your essays and interview. You can convey this quality when responding to typical essay and interview questions that ask for your career goals and why you need an MBA, or what you have learned from a major failure.

Progress: Your progress is most obvious from your resume, which should show your career progression in an easily understandable format. You can also use essays as an opportunity to talk about progress; in fact, most schools explicitly ask you to write about progress as part of your application. Interviewers will also often quiz you about progress early in the interview at the same time as they try to learn about your goals and reasons for attending their MBA program. Progress can also be demonstrated from your undergraduate transcript – if you studied a degree that's relevant to your career goal, that is certainly a form of progress.

Uniqueness: What makes you unique should be apparent from your essays, and during your interview. If you come from a typical background (e.g., finance, consulting), you will want to emphasize your uniqueness. One important way to display uniqueness is in the goals and values of your Mission Statement – if you have done a good job of developing this statement, you should be able to discuss it in a way that makes you sound like an interesting and unique individual. You can also try discussing unique experiences as you address typical essay and interview topics like "maturity" and "leadership." For example, if you are choosing between two stories about leadership, one of which occurred in your home country and one of which occurred during your two years living in sub-equatorial Africa, consider that the African story conveys uniqueness without your ever having to say so. If your background is obviously unique in and of itself (e.g., you have only worked for NGOs), your uniqueness will be evident from your

resume and you may find yourself in the opposite position of arguing that your uniqueness does not make you so different from a typical MBA student that you simply won't fit in.

A Note on Recommendation Letters

Most of the explanations above did not address the use of recommendation letters. That is because, to a large extent, recommendation letters can be used to address whatever qualities you want them to address. If you don't have compelling evidence of intellectual ability from your test scores or work experience, you can try to address this weakness by looking for a recommender who can write about something intellectually challenging you've done. This might not be enough to make you look like a genius, but it might help you avoid looking as though you are intellectually inferior. You can use recommendation letters to address almost any quality – there's no reason why recommenders cannot address your leadership, ethics, or management skills. This concept will be discussed in greater detail below in the section on recommendation letters.

Mapping Your Written Application

Before moving on to the next section of this guide, go through a process of mapping your Admission Case to the different parts of your written application.

When mapping, keep in mind that it is preferable to address each quality reasonably well rather than to do an excellent job of addressing a few qualities while ignoring the others. It is often sufficient to only address each quality once – e.g., if you have excellent scores, there's not much value in trying to prove your intellect in other parts of the application. If you have a great leadership story in one of your essays, you probably have that quality covered, and in other parts of your application you should devote more attention to qualities you have not yet addressed. Of course, it's not bad if you address your leadership or intellect in other parts of the application – and perhaps you should put extra emphasis on leadership if this quality is critical to your Admission Case or if the school you are applying to places extra emphasis on leadership; just don't do so at the cost of completely ignoring other qualities. While business school AdComs understand that you will be stronger in some qualities than others – and even judge you along the maturity quality in part by how aware you are of your weak points – they will become concerned if a number of qualities are simply not well addressed in your application.

Mapping with the *AKAD Excel Worksheet*

It is easy to do your mapping using the *AKAD Excel Worksheet*. Go to the tab labeled "Mapping worksheet." You can write an "X" or other marker in the table on the left side to show which parts of your application will display which qualities. Note that the sheet requires that you be specific about how you will address each part of your Admission Case. For example, don't just plan to address leadership in your essays. Note down exactly what examples of leadership you are going to use in which essay, and what other qualities you can touch on in the same example. You will have to go through this exercise once per school you apply to, because each school is going to ask you different essay questions and will have other minor differences in their applications. Whereas the essays for one school may give you a perfect opportunity to address your management capabilities, you may find that you have to rely more on your resume or a recommendation letter for another school. Note that the *AKAD Excel Worksheet* also allows you to map to your interview, but remember that in most cases you will only get an interview if your written application convinces AdCom that you deserve one, so try to map every quality to somewhere within your written application.

Planning Each Section of Your Application

This section will address each section of your application in turn. As essays are the most complex and difficult piece of the application, more space will be spent on essays than on any other area.

Scores: Not the Be-All and End-All

You cannot change your undergraduate grades. You can, depending on how much time you've allowed yourself, improve your GMAT and (if necessary) TOEFL scores. As there are numerous in-depth books, computer programs, and courses devoted entirely to GMAT and TOEFL, this guide will not dispense much advice except to say:

- Give yourself enough time to re-take your exams in case you have a bad day. Different schools have different policies about multiple exam scores. Most schools will simply accept the highest score you submit, while some will use an average of multiple scores. If you really do terribly the first time you take an exam, even averaging in a better score will be to your advantage. Note, however, that if you don't leave yourself enough time to provide a new set of scores to AdCom in time for the admissions deadline, you won't have any opportunity to improve your chances. If

you are applying in Round 1 for an American program, you will ideally take your exams in the preceding spring, 6 months before you apply.

- Remember that bad scores do not dictate your application success. As described above, your scores only really address a few aspects of the 3Cs model. Applicants tend to focus too much attention on scores because they are the most easily comparable part of the application – I can quickly see that your 700 GMAT score is better than my 650, but I can't easily know if my leadership experience is better than yours. You *can* make up for relatively low scores, especially in the GMAT, if you are strong in other areas. Don't just look at the average GMAT score of your target schools; look at the 80% range.

> *Applicants with 770 GMAT scores routinely get rejected in favor of people with 690s, because the applicants with 770s are relatively weak in other areas where the applicants with 690s are strong.*

If you are within that 80% range, the school is not going to disqualify you simply based on your scores (if you can't find an 80% range but can find the standard deviation, you can easily compute a 65% and a 95% range on your own). However, some schools publish the minimum score that they will accept – if you are below the minimum score a school accepts, look elsewhere.

- Remember that *good* scores also don't dictate your application success. If you have great scores, don't become overconfident. Great scores may or may not be able to offset weaknesses in other areas of your application. People with 770 GMATs routinely get rejected from top MBA programs in favor of people with 690 GMATs, because the applicants with 770s are relatively weak in other areas where the 690s are strong.

- Dress in layers for the exam. Body temperature has an often under-estimated effect on mental acuity and many test centers are not well air-conditioned or heated. You're better off not sleeping the night before an exam than you are taking it in uncomfortably warm or cold conditions. Dress in layers so you can ensure you're comfortable during the exam.

A final note about scores relates back to your undergraduate transcript. While most MBA programs now accept self-reported transcripts during the application process, if you are accepted, you will still need to provide an official copy of your transcript before matriculating. Some undergraduate schools are very responsive in responding to requests for transcripts, while others are extremely slow and disorganized. Make sure to clearly explain the format in which you need your transcript sent – typically, in a sealed envelope, signed or stamped across the seal, sent directly to the school you're applying to. You may also need to arrange for official translations of your transcripts and for conversion to a 4.0 grade scale. These

tasks can take lots of time – so as soon as you get your applications sent, start inquiring at your undergraduate institution about how to go about having your official transcript sent should the need arise.

Resume: Summarizing Yourself

> **Your resume is your best chance to make a good first impression.**

Your resume is often the first part of your application that an AdCom member reviews. It is also often the only part of your application that an interviewer reviews before interviewing you. Therefore, your resume is your best chance to make a good first impression.

A note on definitions is in order here. Typically, in America, a resume is a one-page summary of work and education experience that you make entirely on your own. However, in their application forms, most schools ask you to fill out lists of work experience, educational experience, and other interests – basically adding up to another, longer resume. In recognition of this duplication, a small number of schools no longer request a separate resume as part of the written application because they feel they can get all of the information they need from the lists and charts on the application forms. For the purposes of this section, we will be discussing the more demanding traditional resume that you create by yourself. What is written here can be applied just as well to an application form – except that when filling out an application form, you don't have to worry about issues like formatting.

If you turn back to the application mapping section, you will see that a resume can demonstrate your abilities in many different areas, depending on what experiences you include on it. So as you write your resume, focus on conveying your career progress, but also be on the lookout for opportunities to show your strengths in other areas.

Resume structure

A typical resume has four parts.

- **Identity:** At the top of your resume, you write your name, contact information, and, in many cases a single sentence summary of either who you are ("proven financial analyst with strong team-leading experience") or your purpose ("to gain admission to ABC for an MBA"). Things to keep in mind in this section are:

  o Keep contact information simple. Use one email address, and the one phone number that you will always be using (usually your mobile phone). Also use a single address (or no address at all). Simplicity here not only makes it easier for AdCom to know how to

reach you, it also saves space that can more profitably be used in the other three sections.

- o Do not provide too much personal information. It is considered unprofessional and inappropriate in the USA and most EU countries to list any of the following information on the Identity section of your resume: your gender, age, marital status, religious or political affiliations, or ethnicity. Naturally, some of this information will be evident anyway – if your name is Sarah Zhang, the reviewer will know you're an ethnically Chinese woman. He or she can also guess your age from your college graduation date. If you happen to list activities like "Team Leader, Catholic Volunteer Program" later in your resume, the reviewer can also figure out that you are probably Catholic. All of these situations are unavoidable and not at all problematic. However, it is a problem to explicitly list any of this information in your Identity section.

- *Career:* Your career section usually comes right below your Identity section (though most schools don't mind if you place the Education section above your Career section). In your Career section, you want to list all of the significant jobs you have had, and provide examples of what you did in those jobs.

  - o Use *reverse* chronological order in this section. That is, your current (or most recent) job comes first. The job you held before that comes second, etc. The reason for this ordering is that the reviewer, especially if pressed for time, may only care what the current state of your career progression is, not how you got there.

  - o For every job, provide the company name, your office location, and a brief description of the company's main business (unless the company's full name explains what it does, e.g., First National Bank, or the company is so well known to the general public that there's virtually no chance the reviewer won't already know what the company does, e.g., Coca-Cola Co. Sometimes it is easiest to simply put the web address of the company's main English website). You should also include your most recent title, and the dates at which you worked in this capacity.

  - o If you have had multiple titles within the same company, it is your choice whether to include a separate job entry for each of those titles, or to include them all into one entry. This will probably depend on the differences in responsibility of your different titles, and also in part on space considerations – if you've had many different work experiences, you will have less space to address each title separately.

  - o For each job, include a few bullet points that show not the routine work of this job, but rather your major accomplishments. Use verbs that emphasize your personal

involvement and evidence that quantifies your achievement. Try to keep each bullet point no longer than 2 lines.

- **_Education:_** This section will usually come right after your work experience. Generally, it is expected that you include only higher education – that is, your Bachelor's degree and any graduate degrees. If for some reason you believe it is important to show your high school (perhaps you took a lot more quantitative courses in high school and want to bolster your analysis quality by showing this fact) devote only a small amount of space to that school.

  - Like the career section, this section should be in reverse chronological order and should show the name and location of each school, the time you spent there, your major or concentration, and the degree you earned.

  - For each school, you should include a few bullet points that show information like any scholarships or other honors you were awarded, your GPA (preferably computed in the standard American 4.0 format) and/or class rank, and your major extra-curricular activities.

    > **_Bullet points should show your major accomplishments, not routine work._**

  - Try to portray your GPA in the best possible light. If your in-major GPA is higher than your overall GPA, mention so. If you had a tough first year at college but steadily improved your performance over time, point that out.

  - Also, keep in mind that different schools have different grading standards – in some schools, a 3.0 GPA is unusually high, while in others (especially the big American liberal arts universities that graduate so many future MBA applicants each year), anything less than a 3.0 is poor. Therefore, your class rank is often seen by AdCom as a more objective indicator of your performance than your GPA.

- **_Other:_** This section allows you to describe other factors about yourself that paint you as unique, demonstrate your personal interests, and so on. Generally, this section is viewed as auxiliary to, and should be smaller than, the Career and Education sections. Typical entries in this section are: hobbies, community service, language ability, and other qualifications.

  - You can use this section to convey vital information about qualifications you have. For example, if you are a qualified CFA, this may be the best location on the resume to say so. If you have any publications under your belt, you can mention them here.

○   Also remember that including a few personal interests makes you seem like a more fun person. If AdCom has to choose between a fun person and a boring person, they will choose the fun one. However, personal interests that are seemingly asocial will not help you much. "Reading" or "video games" make you look like a geek with no social life. You'll be better off listing the alternative activities "running a book discussion club" and "organizing gaming contests."

Keep in mind that the total length of your resume should be one page exactly. The overall look should be formal and conservative. The paper should be white and the type face should be easily readable – 10 or 11 point is a good choice. You may see other people creating resumes of two or more pages. If applying to American schools, do not imitate them – as a fairly rigid rule, someone with less than about 15 or 20 years of work experience (a group that includes the vast majority of business school applicants) should not have a resume exceeding a single page. This length rule is looser in Europe; some schools will indicate how long they would like your resume to be.

> *Personal interests that are seemingly asocial will not help you much.*

You will also see people using tiny type faces and other formatting tricks to squeeze huge amounts of information into their resume. This is a bad idea for two reasons. First, it shows a concerning inability to prioritize important information and summarize it into a succinct format (i.e., poor communication skills) and perhaps a certain degree of self-aggrandizement (which may raise questions about your teamwork skills and maturity level). Second, it becomes really hard for anyone to read your resume without hurting their eyes. AdCom members who get a headache from trying to read your application will probably be disinclined to support you (Sloan suggests that resumes be no more than 50 lines long; that is a good upper limit to keep in mind).

You may also hear about "functional" resumes that are not organized in the "Career," "Education," and "Other" style described above, but instead are organized according to your skill sets, e.g., "analytical skills," "management experience," etc. These are usually not preferred by AdCom, who want to be able to quickly scan your resume to see your career progression. Your essays and recommendation letters are more than adequate to fill the role of a "functional" resume.

Resume writing style

There is a specific writing style that must be used in the Career, Education and Other sections of your resume. This writing style has a number of characteristics:

- **Use the correct tense.** This is probably the easiest aspect of the resume writing style.

- The Career and Education sections of your resume should be almost completely written in the simple past tense: e.g., "Organized team to…," "Graduated with degree in…" etc.

- The Other section can often be written in the simple present tense: e.g., "Fluent in English and Spanish," "Enjoy basketball and baseball," etc.

- **Prioritize information extremely.** It is common for a reviewer to spend less than a minute reading your resume. Anytime the reviewer comes across information that seems irrelevant, boring, or unimpressive, they will skip to a point further down the resume. It may be the next bullet, or it may be a point all the way down in the next section. Therefore, you need to think extremely carefully about what information you include, and how you order that information.

  - Put the most important, impressive information first, even at the level of a single bullet point. If you are writing a bullet point about how you led a project team in an analysis of the marketing mix effectiveness of a client company and your

> *It is common for a reviewer to spend less than a minute reading your resume.*

  analysis led to a 10% increased in revenue per marketing dollar, put "Achieved 10% increase in revenue" first and an explanation of the project later in the bullet.

  - Don't include a lot of routine or irrelevant information. If you worked as a consultant, it does not add much to your resume to write "participated in many strategy projects for many clients" or "made strategic analyses and portrayed them in PowerPoint slides." These are just descriptions of routine functions of your job, and are identical to the day to day functions of all other consultants. Look for specific achievements that set you apart from others.

  - Make difficult choices about what information to keep and what to cut. If you have 10 great hobbies, it is better to focus on 2 or 3 than to list all 10. No reviewer will finish reading a 10-point list. They might, however, be willing to read about 2 or 3 activities where you accomplished something interesting.

Use Numbers and Provide Context

I did well in math at college	I scored 90% in college math	I was ranked in top 2% in college math
I worked on a successful efficiency project	I cut 1 hour off production time	I cut 10% off production time
I successfully launched a new product	My product launch sold 10,000 units in its first year	My product launch gained 20% share the first year
Completely Meaningless: not specific	Still lacking context	Concrete!

- ***Use numbers in context to measure your accomplishments.*** Include detailed, contextual and quantitative measures of your accomplishments whenever possible. Don't say "improved sales team performance." This phrase is almost meaningless. Also don't say "Improved sales by $5M." If I'm reading your resume I might not know if $5M is a lot for your company – if you were working at a huge conglomerate, $5M might just be a drop in the bucket; if you are working at a tiny startup, $5M might represent doubled sales. However, if you say "improved performance of six-person sales team by 20% in one year," you give me a lot of context and concrete information with which to evaluate you. Now I know you were supervising six people and that you had a significant, measurable impact on their performance within a relatively short timeframe.

- ***Use verbs that emphasize your actions.*** You want every word on your resume to count, and verbs are among the most important words. You want to suggest qualities like leadership, teamwork, and innovation with your verbs. Don't say "worked on marketing project as head data analyst." Say "led analytical piece of team marketing project." All of a sudden, you are implying a leadership role. Incidentally, the word "team," while not a verb, also suggests teamwork. Instead of "Served as Treasurer of school club," write "Elected Treasurer…" Being elected implies that people like you, which suggests you are strong in qualities like teamwork and communication. Replace "Received award" with "Earned award" or "Won award" to remind the reviewer that it was your abilities, not the kindness of some unknown benefactor, that got you your award.

- *Write understandably.* Do not use highly technical or industry specific language on a resume intended for a business school. Use common business terms. If you cannot explain your job in terms that a reader from another industry can understand effortlessly, then you do not understand your job from a management perspective. Amateurs speak in complex terms to create a façade of expertise. Professionals speak in simple terms to make sure everyone understands what they're saying. Don't write your resume like an amateur would.

It takes several revisions to complete a good resume. Your first few revisions should be focused on deciding what information to include and how to structure that information within each bullet point. As you perfect the information content, you should then focus on perfecting the grammar and spelling. Reviewers are generally quite impatient with basic grammar and spelling errors, which they will assume reflects carelessness and a lack of effort on your part.

A final note about resumes is that you need to be able to speak at length and in detail about every little point on your resume. If you list "group hiking" as one of your interests in your Other section, you had better be ready to talk about your favorite trails, and have one or two stories about great – or disastrous – hikes you've been on. Similarly, if you note in your Education section that you

> *You need to be able to speak at length and in detail about every little point on your resume.*

were awarded first prize in a school-wide business case competition five years ago, you should be able to discuss the business case you submitted, the role of each member of your case team, and so on. Writing something on your resume that you cannot talk about in detail is very risky. If, for example, your interviewer asks you a detailed question about the seemingly least important point on your resume and you can't easily answer it, he will immediately begin to suspect that you have fabricated it (and it will be very hard to allay this suspicion once it has arisen). If you have fabricated one small, unimportant point, it is easy to imagine that you fabricated the big, important points too.

Example of a bad resume

A sample essay, by "Joe Li" is included on page 84. What's bad about Joe's resume? Almost everything. Below is a list of the major problems.

- The Identity section contains too much contact information, which will be confusing to anyone who wants to reach Joe. This section also contains a lot of information that should not be there at all, such as gender and race. The result is that the space left for the Career and Education sections is smaller than it should be.

- The Education section comes prior to the Career section, even though Joe graduated 5 years ago. This is forgivable in an MBA application (but would be less forgivable if Joe were to use the same resume to apply for a job).

- The Career section is in chronological order, instead of *reverse* chronological order.

- The Other section header is inexplicably of a different format than the Career and Education section headers.

- Within the Career section, job headings are not clear – it is not immediately apparent what some companies do, and it is hard to find the years where Joe worked in each position.

- The nature of Geewhiz Technology's work is completely unclear.

- Punctuation is erratic, with some bullets ending with a full stop and others having no punctuation at all.

- Information is poorly prioritized; for example, the first bullet for Poseidon spends a full line of text talking about ship utilization before mentioning that Joe increased the net profit of the company by 3%.

- Joe presents lists, such as the list of countries he's visited and sports he's interested in, which most reviewers will never bother to read.

- Many claims are poorly supported by evidence, such as the first point at Cashbag, which says he received "strong" performance reviews. Readers of this resume will wonder "how strong?" and "when?"

- Verbs do not create the impression that Joe was doing anything other than low level analytical and support work. For example, the 2nd and 3rd bullet in Cashbag say that Joe "participated" and "helped." In fact, in one project he was lead analyst and in the other he was lead modeler.

- Overall formatting is ugly.

Joe Li

Home: +852 5555 5555; Mobile: +852 9555 9555/+86 139 9666 6666; Office: +852 4444 4444
Email: email@email.com / workemail@workemail.com
Apartment 7F, Block 3, Sunrise Vista, 44 Caine Road, Midlevels, Hong Kong

Gender: Male   Date of Birth: June 6 1982
Race: Chinese   Marital Status: Single

Education

Peking University, Beijing, China
Earned BBA from Guanghua in 2004
- Magna cum Laude, 3.4 GPA
- 3rd place in English speaking contest
- As president of finance club, established annual conference with Tsinghua, JiaoDa and Fudan universities.
- Vice president of mountain eagles club; planned team climbing expeditions
- Wrote thesis on China SOE banking reform and its impact on HK equity markets

Work Experience

Geewhiz Technology, Shanghai, China
Intern, summer 2004
- Helped make powerpoint presentations for management
- Researched potential cooperative partners.

Cashbag Bank, Hong Kong, China
Analyst, 2004-2006
- Received strong performance reviews
- Performed modeling and presentations for Poseidon Europa IPO as lead analyst. Offering was 50% oversubscribed.
- Assisted in Hanbak Clothing's $500 million debt issuance.
- Marketed to a number of corporations considering equity or debt issuances by performing industry research and creating presentations.

Poseidon Europa International Shipping, Shanghai, China
Senior Planner, 2006-Present
- Developed fleet utilization methodology that improved utilization by 1.5% and led to 3% increase in net profits.
- Participated in due diligence of proposed purchase of 2 $50 million ships
- Helped plan SEA market entry, which achieved very solid growth and earned management praise.

Other

- Native speaker of Mandarin and Shanghainese, excellent English, once took a course in German
- Basketball (love the NBA), soccer, mountain climbing, and bowling.
- Have travelled to Hong Kong, Singapore, Kuala Lumpur, Indonesia, North Korea, and Vietnam.

JOE LI
+852 9555 5555
email@email.com

EXPERIENCE

POSEIDON EUROPA INTERNATIONAL SHIPPING CORPORATION   Shanghai, China
Senior Planner – Planning Department   2006 – Present
- Increased net profits by 3% by creating new management system that improved utilization by 1.5%.
- Prevented corporation from overinvesting in fleet assets during due diligence into proposed purchase of 2 $50 million used "panamax" container ships; correctly projected decrease in shipping demand.
- Selected market niches to enter during move into South East Asia market; growth exceeded management expectations by 5%.
- Lead internal analyst in Poseidon's $20 million acquisition of Sarong Shipping Corporation.
- Maintained positive relations with multi-lingual and multi-cultural management and clients.
- Organized and gave training in financial modeling for planning department staff.
- All work performed in English.

CASHBAG BANK INCORPORATED   Hong Kong, China
Analyst – Investment Banking Division   2004 - 2006
- Lead analyst on Poseidon Europa International Shipping Corporation's successful $750 million initial public offering in Hong Kong. Offering was 50% oversubscribed.
- Completed modeling for successful $500 million debt issuance by Hanbak Clothing Corporation.
- Consistently earned ratings in top 20% of analyst class.
- Created "analyst social fund" and organized several social events for other analysts.

GEEWHIZ TECHNOLOGY (Green energy startup)   Shanghai, China
Intern – International Business Development   Summer 2004
- Pursued international partnership potential with European green energy companies.
- Authored English presentation materials for international investors.

EDUCATION

GUANGHUA SCHOOL OF MANAGEMENT, PEKING UNIVERSITY   Beijing, China
Bachelor of Business Administration – International Finance   2000 - 2004
- Magna cum Laude; 3.4 GPA, 3.85 within major.
- Won 3rd place in campus-wide English speaking contest with self-authored speech.
- Elected president of finance club; established annual finance conference with leading universities.
- Elected vice-president for expedition planning of "Mountain Eagles" mountain climbing club; planned and financed 2-week climbing expeditions for teams of 30.
- Earned "China Everbright" scholarship for demonstrated academic excellence and leadership.

ADDITIONAL INFORMATION

- **Languages**: Native speaker of Mandarin and Shanghainese. Excellent business English.
- **Sports**: Mountain climbing – have led expeditions up 4 of China's 5 famous peaks.
- **Travel**: Enjoy traveling off the beaten path, e.g., have toured North Korea.

Above is a much improved version of the same resume. Take a close look and see how the problems described above have been corrected. Additionally, the following two changes have been made:

- The resume now mentions activities that demonstrate qualities like innovation and involvement, such as Joe's establishment of training at Poseidon and activity leadership at Cashbag.

- Because Joe is not a native speaker of English, he now emphasizes that much of his work experience has been performed in English.

Essays: Not Just Good Writing

Your essays, with the possible exception of preparation for standardized tests like the GMAT, are the part of your application that should take the most time and focus. Not only does each individual essay consume time as you structure, write, re-write and edit it, but because different schools ask different essay questions and impose different length requirements, you have to partially or completely re-write the essays for each school you apply to.

General writing advice

There are a number of points to keep in mind when writing your business school essays.

- ***Write them yourself.*** You may hate writing, you may think you're a terrible writer, or you may be very busy. If so, you may face a temptation either to have someone else draft your essays for you, or to copy partial or complete essays off the internet. There are three reasons this is a bad idea.

  o Quality: The essay questions for business schools require personal stories backed up with a great deal of specific evidence and self-reflection. To be effective, this kind of content must come from you. No one else knows exactly what you felt that time you caught your manager cheating on client expenses, or when the

  > *If you are discovered cheating in the application process, your chances of getting in are forever destroyed.*

  conference you had been planning for 10 months was cancelled due to a hurricane. And essays that lack this level of specificity and detail will be boring and generic, and will not get you accepted. Maybe if you spend a lot of time telling someone else about these experiences in great detail they could write about them effectively – but if you're going to spend that much time conveying the story orally, you might as well write it yourself.

o Risk: You are likely to be caught. AdCom may recognize that parts of your essay were copied from someone else's. Or when you interview, whatever your ghostwriter wrote for you probably won't be quite what you tell the interviewer – setting off alarm bells. Obviously, if you are discovered cheating in the application process, your chances of getting in are forever destroyed.

o Ethics: It is wrong to cheat in the admissions process.

- **Don't make stuff up.** For reasons similar to the point above, you should not fabricate experiences for your essays. You probably cannot write with convincing detail and feeling about something that never happened, you are likely to get caught, and it's wrong. Don't worry if other applicants have bigger achievements. MBA AdComs are primarily interested in what you can achieve in the future. What you have achieved in the past is only interesting to them in as much as it shows something about you along the 3Cs. You may have displayed more innovation, leadership and communication skills in attaining a relatively minor success than someone else did in attaining a seemingly much larger success, and it's the innovation, leadership and communication that AdCom cares about, not the success itself. That being said, do feel free to use a little poetic license. For example, maybe you didn't really have any clear career goals when you took that first job in finance, but it's fine to say in your essays that you took it with the purpose of learning X, Y and Z skills that will be valuable to your long term career goals.

- **Write multiple drafts.** It is often hard to achieve the necessary levels of focus and articulation in your first couple of attempts to write an essay. Many people find it helpful to write a relatively long first draft (e.g., 1,200 to 1,500 words for a 1,000-word essay) and to come back later and streamline the essay into a more focused, shorter piece. After writing the draft, put it away for a few days before coming back to edit it yourself. Editing something you just wrote – especially if you need to cut its length significantly – is a painful process, and you will probably be able to wield your editor's red pen far more objectively if you first let some time pass.

- **Get editing input.** While you should not let anyone else write your essays, you should ask others (whether friends, colleagues, or professional application consultants) to read them and give you editing input. After you receive their edits, consider if you agree with the changes they have suggested. Rewrite the changes yourself to ensure that the essay remains in your own voice. Only directly accept

> *How do you think a busy, stressed out AdCom member operating under tight deadlines will react to a candidate who has decided he is so important that the essay length requirements don't apply to him?*

edits if they are corrections to grammar, spelling and word-choice.

- ***Honor length requirements.*** Put yourself in the shoes of AdCom members. They have to read dozens of applications each day. They assign essay length requirements so that they are not completely overwhelmed. How do you think a busy, stressed out AdCom member operating under tight deadlines will react to a candidate who has decided he is so important that the essay length requirements don't apply to him? Right – they will react with hostility. Don't make AdCom members angry at you. Keep them happy by staying within their essay length guidelines. (If you are still tempted to exceed word limits, consider that some schools use computers to automatically truncate overly long essays to the word limit!)

- ***Try to use a narrative structure.*** In each of your application essays, you want to get across a small number of points that address some of the qualities in the 3Cs model. As much as possible, you want to avoid lists when making these points. Instead, you should aim to tie the points together into a single narrative, where one point leads logically to the next. As will be discussed below, many of your essay responses will consist of a large analytical section, and this analysis may be hard to structure as a narrative, unless you are an unusually gifted writer. However, most essays also consist of

Real World Example

Applicants often struggle the most with essays that are open-ended and leave the content totally up to the applicant. A classic example is the Chicago Booth requirement that each applicant submit an "essay" comprised of 4 PowerPoint slides about anything.

Many applicants react to this requirement by making 4 slides of small-font bullet points detailing all their qualities and accomplishments. This approach is likely to bore AdCom more than impress them.

We have helped applicants take a step back and think about how this unusual essay fits into their overall application. This essay should be designed to emphasize a few key points about the applicant, as if the applicant were using it to create a brand for themselves.

The applicants first must decide which are the key points they want to present in their brand. They may want to focus their brand around their Mission Statement. Or perhaps they have a few qualities that really define them and they want to focus their brand on these.

The 4 slide presentation emphasizes the need to find a tight narrative focus and purpose for each essay. If you don't, you will get the essay equivalent of unreadable, dense lists of bullet points.

a "setup" and an "action" section. These sections can often easily be structured as a narrative; i.e., the story of what happened and why. The narrative structure of a story is an excellent approach for three main reasons:

- Human brains respond very well to narratives. Well-written stories are easy for the reader to remember, and can be very engaging on an emotional level;

- A story develops a small number of ideas over its length and leads to a clear conclusion about each idea;

- The discipline of planning and sticking to a clear narrative forces you, the writer, to clarify your thoughts.

- **Open up.** Many candidates become worried that if they write something truly personal in their essays, they will be deemed unprofessional or unconventional by AdCom. This is not the case; in fact, AdCom members are tired of reading endless piles of essays that all try to seem "conventional." "Conventional" essays are boring and unmemorable. Be courageous enough to open up to your reader, as you might to an intimate friend. There's no reason to be shy: your essays (and other application materials) are confidential documents and will not be shared.

- **Stay recent, stay in the real world.** Try to focus as many essays as possible on experiences that occurred in the last 4 or 5 years. Similarly, focus on "real world" experiences at work more than on experiences that date back to your college or (even worse) high school days. While it is fine to refer to one or two early or academic experiences in your essays, if you do so repeatedly, AdCom members may assume that you have no recent, real world experiences, which implies you have not had a very successful and progress-filled career in recent years.

- **Remember your audience.** Remember that your audience members, by virtue of serving on AdCom, are probably quite interested in stories of human development. They are fascinated by stories of applicants' personal development, life goals, values, and so on. They will naturally understand applicants who can speak to them in such terms. They will probably not be impressed by applicants who try to show off their expertise by using lots of business buzz words, acronyms, and technical terminology. In fact, if you write in highly technical terms specific to your industry, you may simply confuse or alienate AdCom members who lack a background in your field.

> *AdCom will probably not be impressed by applicants who try to show off their expertise by using lots of business buzzwords, acronyms, and technical terminology.*

- *Focus on why, not just what.* Remember that AdCom members are trying to understand (among other things) what your goals are, what your values are, what motivates you, and how you think and react in different situations. Therefore, simply writing about what your career goals are or what you did that time two of your team members were fighting does not satisfy AdCom's desire for information about you. If you only write about the what, AdCom members may decide you are boring. They may also assume that you are weak in terms of maturity because you have not demonstrated an ability to self-reflect. Focus on the greater purpose, the values, and the reasoning behind your goals, decisions and actions.

- *Keep on message and paint a consistent picture.* While you will be mapping your essays to portray different qualities, keep in mind that you have to keep a consistent image of yourself across essays. You cannot, for instance, compose one essay that discusses how you rose above abject poverty during your youth, and another essay saying that your interest in finance first arose as you grew up watching your father, an investment banker, help mid-sized businesses grow. The disconnection between having a father in a high-income career and overcoming poverty will be confusing for AdCom members. They will probably decide that you are writing fiction. Keep your Admission Case in mind as you plan out your essays – everything you write must stay on the message of your Admission Case.

- *Be aware of and avoid violating cultural taboos.* America may be an open society, but it has many very clear taboo subjects. Universities are their own microcosm of American society and have their own unique taboos. Violating these taboos can easily get you rejected. Especially for foreign applicants, understanding the taboos within the rarified culture of elite American universities can be challenging. Some key taboos to keep in mind as you write your essays include:

  o *Gender:* Never indicate that you believe there is any difference in the capabilities or emotional states of men and women. Refer to women as "women," not "girls."

  o *Race:* Never indicate that you believe there are any significant differences in mental or physical capabilities, or in cultural sophistication, of different races or ethnic groups. Always use accepted, polite terminology for racial and ethnic groups. There are many terms for different ethnic groups that you may have heard used frequently in American movies or songs but that are absolutely unacceptable for you to use. Some proper terms are:

    ▪ *Westerners:* White or Caucasian

    ▪ *Asians:* Asian, Asian-American

90

- **Blacks:** Black, African, African-American

  o **Religion:** Religion is a nuanced subject in America. Never mock the religious beliefs of any group. Feel free to refer to your own religious beliefs if they are important to you and relevant to your application, but do not appear to be advocating your own beliefs over those of anyone else.

  o **Sexuality:** Never appear critical of anyone for their personal lifestyles (e.g., homosexuality).

  o **Family background:** Americans are generally neither impressed by high status family backgrounds, nor put off by low status family backgrounds. In fact, you may find that Americans are generally more impressed with people from low status backgrounds who have managed to succeed than they are with any other group; and may even be dismissive of accomplishments of people from high status family backgrounds. Therefore, do not brag about your family background. Do not be dismissive of others due to their backgrounds. (In Europe, this taboo is usually not as strong.)

  o **Outsourcing:** Business decisions that save companies money by moving their production outsourcing operations to low-cost locations like China are highly sensitive in America, where such decisions lead to Americans losing their jobs. Business school AdCom members generally understand the business logic, but may still have negative emotional reactions to these decisions.

  o **Domestic politics:** In America, it is simply considered unprofessional to discuss domestic politics in any business setting. There is a very simple reason: domestic politics are fraught with emotion and you may offend someone unintentionally.

Unfortunately, there are too many cultural taboos, and each one is too nuanced, for them all to be covered within this guide. Getting an American to read over your application before submission and judge it for "cultural sensitivity" is a great idea.

You may be applying for MBA degrees in other countries besides America. While the specifics will differ, most of the taboos above will hold across North America, Europe and any MBA program that is heavily influenced by Western educational philosophy, even including institutions like CEIBS in China.

Essay question models

Before you write your essays, you need to understand the purpose behind each essay question. Luckily, most essay questions fit into one or more of the 11 model essay questions below. Once you can classify

an essay question as being of a certain model, or as being a combination of more than one model, you can quickly focus on the qualities most relevant to the essay, and begin structuring your response based on the evidence you have already compiled for those qualities as part of your Communication Strategy. Below are the 11 models that *most* essay questions will fit into. (Note that many essay questions will be a combination of 2 or more models.)

Most of the model questions directly address one or two qualities: e.g., leadership, goals, and innovation. (There is one exception: the "Mentor" model does not directly address any one or two qualities, but rather addresses several at once.) Clearly, you absolutely must focus on the quality or qualities addressed by an essay question as you respond to it. In addition to any qualities directly addressed, there are always additional qualities that you can easily address in your responses to that model question. Exactly which qualities you address in each essay will largely depend on what examples you use and what stories you tell, though the guide below suggests the most obvious and easily included qualities for each model. As you map out your essay responses to your Admission Case, make sure to make use of opportunities to address multiple qualities in each essay.

> **In terms of structure, most essay models can be split 20/40/40.**

In terms of structure, most essay models can best be split 20/40/40: 20% of the length should be an explanation of the situation you are writing about. For example "I had joined XYZ corporation only 3 months ago and was already asked to manage a team of 6 staff in repairing a disastrous customer relationship with a key client..." 40% of the essay should be a description of the actions you took and decisions you made, as well as the reasoning underlying your actions and decisions. For example "I decided to start by interviewing XYZ staff who had been working with the client in question to learn about how the relationship went bad. Then I set up a meeting with the client's CEO to present some ideas about how the relationship could be improved..." The last 40% should be an analysis of the outcomes, of what your actions reveal about you, and of what you learned from the experience. For example: "From the failure of my first meeting with the CEO I learned that communicating is often more about listening than speaking..."

This 20/40/40 split does not mean that in a 1,000 word essay, the first 200 words should be spent on situation, the next 400 on action, etc. Instead, these are indications of about how much emphasis and space you should devote to different parts of the story. If you are a gifted writer, you may find it easy to interweave the "action" and "analysis" parts of the story into a single narrative in a very effective way. And perhaps in one essay, the initial situation is so complex you need to devote 1/3 of your space to describing it, leaving less space for "action" and "analysis." Start with the structural guidelines in mind, but don't live and die by them.

Innovation

Examples

- Describe how you solved a complex problem.
- Describe a time you were innovative.

Other Qualities

- Management, teamwork, domain skills, communication, leadership, determination, uniqueness.

Strategy and Structure

- This type of question lets you show many other qualities because it is rare that you can implement an innovation without involving other people.
- Structure should be 20% setup, 40% action, and 40% analysis.

Common Errors

- Focusing on innovation without providing context and analysis.
- Using examples of "artistic" creativity rather than business-oriented innovation.
- Using highly technical language (for example, when describing your solution to an engineering problem.)

Business school AdCom members want to see that you have the problem-solving ability, mental flexibility, and overall creativity to overcome difficult challenges and develop innovations. However, coming up with an idea without executing it (or ensuring that someone else executes it) is not valuable in business, so as a part of this essay, you need to discuss not only how you developed your solution or innovation, but also how you implemented and applied it.

Stories about applied innovation, i.e., problem solving, offer an opportunity to talk about a number of other qualities. Uniqueness and domain skills are often apparent in how you approach the innovation/problem-solving process. You may have used cooperative, leadership or communication skills while putting together a team to help you find your innovation/solution, or when convincing others to adopt it. Finally, your discipline in seeing your ideas through to the end shows your determination and management capability.

Leadership

Examples

- Describe a leadership experience.
- Tell us about your leadership style.
- Describe a time you've mentored or taught others.

Other Qualities

- Teamwork, innovation, management, communication, determination, involvement.

Strategy and Structure

- Describe a time when you led other people to do something they otherwise would not have done. Especially impressive are examples were not in a formal leadership position but instead led through your own initiative, charisma, and force of personality; or when the people you led started off as hostile towards you or your goals.
- Structure should be 20% setup, 40% action, and 40% analysis.

Common Errors

- Confusing leadership with management.
- Forgetting that leadership is about motivating or cultivating others, not oneself.

Business schools pride themselves on turning out leaders, and they will often require you to demonstrate your leadership abilities in your essays. The key to approaching this essay is to clearly understand what leadership means in the eyes of AdCom. Typically this means directly and purposefully influencing others to behave in a way they otherwise would not, though different schools have different philosophies about leadership.

Often, effective leadership relies on strong cooperative and communication skills – e.g., leaders often need to understand team dynamics as they work to get a group of people to work towards a common goal. While acting as a leader, you may also display management skills or determination, especially if you are leading a long or complex endeavor. Leaders often rise to their positions because they have a solution to a problem or an innovative idea, so a leadership essay may allow you to address innovation, too. Leadership essays are a potential area to demonstrate involvement if you have a relevant example from your volunteer experiences.

Communication and Teamwork

Examples

- Describe a time when you faced a conflict on a team or made an unpopular decision.
- Describe a time when you had difficult communicating.

Other Qualities

- Maturity, innovation, leadership, involvement.

Strategy and Structure

- Talk about a time you needed to rely on teamwork or communication with others to achieve a goal or gain support for an unpopular decision. Emphasizing your ability to see others' perspectives and to use tools like negotiations, persuasion, clear communications or compromise to succeed is key.
- Structure should be 20% setup, 40% action, and 40% analysis.

Common Errors

- Failing to show you understood others' perspectives, using methods not consistent with teamwork and communication to get your way.
- Focusing too much on the obstacle, and too little on how you overcame it.

Teamwork and communication skills are necessary for any business leader. The key to this essay is to show not only that you can cooperate and communicate in normal, familiar circumstances, but also in unusual or even extreme circumstances. A story about teamwork or communication that involves hostile personalities, intercultural conflicts, or other obvious challenges is naturally more impressive than one that does not.

This essay model is an excellent opportunity to display your maturity – e.g., after a period of frustration, you realized that you were having trouble working with your project team members or communicating with your client not just because they had personality or communication problems, but because you yourself were doing something to make interactions more difficult. Showing that you have the ability to see yourself in the eyes of others is a sign not only of strong teamwork and communication skills, but also of exceptional maturity. Cooperation and communication essay models also often let you talk about leadership – maybe you rose to a leadership role in that team after you resolved the personality conflicts;. There is often an element of innovation demonstrated in your search for solutions to the

teamwork or communication challenge you describe in this essay.   And especially for young applicants whose work often consists of independent research and analytical work, looking for examples of communication and teamwork from your involvement in your community can sometimes be easier than looking for examples from work.

Involvement

Examples
- How have you contributed to a community?
- How would you like to contribute to our campus outside of the classroom?

Other Qualities
- Leadership, teamwork, ethics, uniqueness.

Strategy and Structure
- If you have substantial community service experience, describe it, what you have learned from it, and how you plan to continue your service during and after business school. If you do not have a substantial experience, you need to think of how to portray something you've done as a form of involvement, e.g., the time you taught the intern how to use PowerPoint demonstrates your interest in teaching others, which you would like to further pursue by participating in the campus tutoring program.
- Structure should be 20% setup, 40% action, and 40% analysis.

Common Errors
- Using an experience that was obviously manufactured for the purpose of writing this essay, e.g., "last week I went to the soup kitchen and learned how rewarding it is to help others…"
- Not tying your past involvement to your MBA campus.

Many business schools, especially North American ones, place a significant value on involvement. This interest does not necessarily derive from a belief that there is any correlation between involvement and business success. It seems instead to be derived from a cultural belief in the value of community involvement, a practical belief that the campus community will be richer if students get actively involved in it, and a calculated belief that the school will have a better reputation if its alumni have contributed to their communities.

AdCom can also use involvement as a lens into other qualities like ethics and teamwork. In terms of ethics, involvement can demonstrate that you care about issues greater than your own advancement. In terms of teamwork, involvement demonstrates that you are willing to give to your community. If you have initiated or led any community or volunteer activities, you can demonstrate leadership here. Also, your involvement says something about your likes and beliefs, and can thereby help communicate your uniqueness quality.

Ethics

Examples

- Describe a moral dilemma you have faced.
- Tell us about a time you observed unethical behavior.

Other Qualities

- Innovation, teamwork, communication, maturity.

Strategy and Structure

- Provide a story that illustrates your willingness and ability to act on your ethical beliefs in difficult situations, e.g., when you could be punished for acting ethically or when you face a true moral dilemma.
- Structure should be 20% setup, 40% action, and 40% analysis.

Common Errors

- Using a moral dilemma that is not a true dilemma, e.g., "to steal or not to steal" is not a dilemma because stealing is always wrong. A good dilemma might be "to be loyal to my company or to do what's best for the client."
- Believing that ethical behavior in normal situations – where there is no special risk, conflict, or temptation – is evidence of strong ethics.
- Finding ethical fault in, and making a fuss about, a very minor issue.

Business schools have a somewhat problematic relationship with ethics. On the one hand, it is terrible for their reputation every time a graduate is caught in an ethics scandal. On the other hand, they do not see it as their role to instill strict ethical codes in their students. Therefore, AdCom members want to see applicants who act according to their own well-developed ethical sense. So the key to this model of essay is not to show that you act in strict accordance to some objective ethical code, but rather to show that you are capable of making your own ethical decisions when confronting complex or difficult ethical situations. Thus, writing an essay about how you never steal will not impress AdCom members.

Discussing how you reacted when you accidentally saw confidential salary files showing that one colleague was getting paid much less than another for doing the same job might impress AdCom members, as long as you do a good job of explaining the competing ethical claims and how you weighed them.

Introspective essays about tough ethical choices display a high level of maturity. Resolving ethical conflicts can also display your innovation, and communicating your opinions can be a stiff test of your communication ability. Note that writing an essay about how you made a tiny or debatable ethical violation into a huge issue may actually harm you along the teamwork quality. For example, writing about the time you convinced cafeteria workers at your company to go on strike because your company was not using "fair-trade coffee beans" is probably not a good idea.

Maturity

Examples
- Describe a failure or mistake and what you learned from it.
- Describe your strengths and weaknesses.

Other Qualities
- Goals, determination.

Strategy and Structure
- Be honest about discussing real failures and weaknesses. For failure stories, the more spectacular and public the failure, the better. But do not forget to discuss what you have done or will do to address your failure or weaknesses.
- Structure should be 20% setup, 40% action, and 40% analysis for failure stories; 50% strengths, 30% weaknesses and 20% how you are addressing the weaknesses for strengths and weaknesses stories.

Common Errors
- Refusing to admit weaknesses or failures; trying to put the blame on someone else; using phony failures and weaknesses ("I work too hard," "my B+ grade on that exam was a failure according to my standards.")
- Failing to analyze and present a plan for rectifying failures and weaknesses.

The maturity essay model typically centers on your failures or weaknesses. The key here is not to duck the question. If AdCom asks for a story about failure, you should write about a time when you publicly

messed up, and caused quantifiable damage or hardship to an organization or goal. Failing an exam in college is not a failure from this perspective, and neither is getting drunk and making a fool of yourself at a friend's wedding. A "good" failure is presenting a report filled with faulty reasoning that causes the client to terminate the project, or ignoring a personality conflict on your project team until two employees quit and the project is ruined. But a good failure story must also include a component of how you reacted to that failure (by acknowledging your mistake and taking the lead to fix the problem you caused, of course) and what you learned from it. Weaknesses should follow the same model – "working too hard" is a cop out. A real weakness is "not being good at managing multiple work streams" or "having trouble developing good marketing concepts for the gadgets I invent." Weaknesses you present should be real, but addressable, and you should detail the ways you are addressing or will address them.

A story of failure is a good time to display determination – i.e., when everyone was aghast at the failure, you stood up and started to fix it. Discussing your weaknesses is a good opportunity to discuss your goals and why addressing your weaknesses is important to achieving your goals.

Uniqueness

Examples
- What is most important to you?
- Describe yourself as an individual.

Other Qualities
- Goals, maturity, teamwork, ethics, involvement.

Strategy and Structure
- Use this essay as a chance to talk about what makes you a unique individual and what you can contribute to campus beyond showing up for class.   Try to paint yourself as someone who is interesting, friendly and social if there is an opportunity to do so.   But ensure that you do talk about things that are important to, or defining of, you, or your essay will be transparently fake.
- You have a lot of freedom in your response, and can vary the structure as you like.

Common Errors
- Trying to be too conventional, not opening up and sharing things that are truly interesting about yourself.
- Trying to say too many things instead of conveying a few key points.

The uniqueness essay model often takes a general approach of asking you to describe your personality. This very open format can make this model tough to answer. It is important to stay focused and not get caught in the trap of trying to portray every facet of your personality. It is also important to understand that there is no right answer to this essay – the whole point of it is to learn about what makes you unique – so trying to make up an answer is pointless. Write honestly. Most efforts to fake responses to questions like this are transparent.

These essays are a good chance to show your teamwork quality – specifically, your ability to get along with other people in a social capacity. If you can link your involvement or self-description to your goals, you will reinforce them in the mind of the reader and possibly come across as a more focused – and therefore, mature – applicant. You can also look for opportunities to describe your ethical values and involvement, especially if you have a concrete commitment to community service that you can describe.

Goals, Effort and Progress

Examples

- Describe your career to date and plans for the future.
- Why do you want an MBA at this time?

Other Qualities

- Maturity, uniqueness, determination, domain skills.

Strategy and Structure

- Base your essay around your Mission Statement. What are your goals? Why? How far have you pursued them? How would an MBA help?
- Consider using a narrative, in which you explain why and how you have your goal, and explain the last several years of your life in terms of pursuing this goal. Then turn to your developmental needs and how this school will help you meet those needs. Conclude with thoughts about how you will contribute to campus life.

Common Errors

- Professing goals which are not legitimate, but which you believe will impress (even if this works in the essay, it probably won't during the interview.)
- Not specifically tailoring the "Why MBA" part of the story to the school in question.
- Writing a life story instead of a goals story.
- Focusing on "what" instead of "why" and "how."

The goals, effort and progress essay model is often the centerpiece of the essay set – it is the first question and has the longest word limit. Luckily, you already built the basic model for responding to this question model back when you created your Mission Statement. Remember to use your Mission Statement as the basic structure of answering this essay. Generally, it is ideal to establish your career goals early in the essay and explain how your education, work, and extra-curricular activities to date comprise progress towards these goals. This creates a narrative flow that helps the reader make sense of your different experiences.

In most of these essays, you should also ensure that you cover two additional points in addition to your goals themselves. The first is explaining why you want to go to this particular school. This is where you

show effort. Do not waste valuable space remarking upon generic issues like the "rigorous academic program" and "excellent industry reputation" of your favorite school. You will be better off if you can speak to specific programs and cultural aspects of each campus: "As you can see from my career goals, financial and entrepreneurial skills, plus a strong intercultural communication ability, are very important to my future success. Therefore I want to go to Wharton because it not only has extremely strong finance and entrepreneurial programs, but it is also the most international top tier MBA program in America, as evidenced by the Lauder Program and its exchange programs with schools like INSEAD and LBS." Or "The small class-size at Stanford sets it apart from other top American programs, and this is exactly the type of intimate, tightly knit environment in which I could build the kinds of personal relationships I will need in my career…"

However, either of these statements alone would not be nearly specific enough to get you points for effort. They would merely be a good starting point. To really show effort, you need to link specific courses or programs at the school with specific areas of learning you need to fill: "I would love to take Professor Smith's course on *Financing LBOs in Developing Markets*, because the module on debt financing in Eastern Europe would really strengthen my understanding of how to run commercial banking operations in former Soviet Republics. I spoke to a current student named Mark Lee who took this course and he assured me this module had exactly the kind of training I want."

The second area you usually need to add into this essay is how you can contribute to the campus community. This is an opportunity to talk about what makes you unique, for one thing, and also to mention any community service activities you have a demonstrable commitment to. "I have been involved in tutoring disadvantaged children since high school, and I noticed that the HBS 'Youth Mentoring Club' is involved in this type of activity. I would love to be able to continue my involvement in tutoring at the YMC." Note that you do not need to touch this topic here if you are addressing it in a separate uniqueness or involvement essay.

Additionally, you can show maturity and determination in your goals essay by showing that you have goals and a clear understanding of what will be necessary to attain them, and have already overcome obstacles in your path to achieving them. There are also many ways you can demonstrate domain skills in this essay, as you discuss your education and work experience.

AKAD MBA Application Guide
www.akadgroup.com

Determination

Examples

- Describe a difficult situation you have faced.
- Which two accomplishments are you most proud of?

Other Qualities

- Maturity, innovation, goals, leadership, uniqueness, progress.

Strategy and Structure

- Describe a story where you overcame substantial obstacles to achieve a goal (which may or may not be related to your career goal; it is possible to write a powerful determination essay about an important personal goal like losing weight or overcoming shyness.)
- Structure should be 20% setup, 40% action, and 40% analysis.

Common Errors

- Not openly discussing any weaknesses that made the situation especially challenging and final success especially rewarding.
- Not explaining the reason for your determination (i.e., what your goals were and why they were valuable to you.)

Determination is important to AdCom members because it shows that you have the tenacity to achieve in the face of challenges. The keys to this essay are to focus on the level of determination you demonstrated, not on the size of the eventual success. You may be able to write a much more impressive essay about a seemingly small and personal success where you overcame difficult challenges – mastering a phobia, learning a new skill, etc.; – than you can about the time you made a $1 million sale to a client with whom you already had an existing personal relationship.

The reason you needed so much determination to complete these goals is often that you needed to overcome a personal weakness. Admitting these weaknesses demonstrates maturity. You will often have demonstrated innovation while overcoming the challenges you faced. Moreover, your story may be tied to your career goals and therefore reinforce your passion about these goals or show how you have fought to make progress towards them. In many cases, your own determination to achieve certain goals helps you become a more effective leader. Or the goals you were pursuing, even if not related to your career goals, may help demonstrate your uniqueness.

Mentors

Examples

- Who has been the greatest influence on your career or life?
- If you could spend a day with one person, who would you choose?

Other Qualities

- Goals, teamwork, ethics, uniqueness, maturity, domain skills.

Strategy and Structure

- This model question is similar to the uniqueness model in that you can use it to show what makes you unique, and how you relate to other people. You should consider linking this mentor to your goals.
- Structure should be 50% describing this person and why you admire them, and 50% a discussion of how you apply their example to your life or what you want to learn from them.

Common Errors

- Being afraid to be unconventional; making a "safe" choice instead of an honest one.
- Not showing enough self-awareness as to why you choose this person, and how this choice reflects your values, interests and goals.

The mentor essay is an attempt by AdCom to learn about your goals, uniqueness, and ethics from a different, somewhat indirect perspective. Before writing this essay, think about which of these qualities you want to focus on the most. If you feel you need to talk more about your goals, write about a mentor or exemplar who has an obvious connection to your career goals. (Note that depending on how the essay question is structured, you may or may not be able to write about someone you don't know personally.) If you think you are a pretty typical applicant (e.g., you are from an investment banking background), you might want to use this essay to emphasize your uniqueness or ethical values more by talking about a person with a slightly more tangential relationship to your career but a direct relationship to some other aspect of your personality you have not yet fully addressed in other essays.

If the essay question is structured to allow it, it can be valuable to discuss your personal relationship with a mentor you actually know – doing so emphasizes your relationship-building ability, part of teamwork. Providing an introspective discussion of why you so admire this individual can also

demonstrate self-knowledge, part of maturity. You can also show domain skills if you can write intelligently about someone important in your chosen field.

What to do with the "extra" essay

Many schools will give you an optional essay, which typically has a relatively short word limit and is phrased something like "If there is anything additional about yourself that you have not had a chance to address in this application, please share it here." Or "If there are any extenuating circumstances in your application, please let us know." The key word here is "*if*." You should write this essay *if* you really have something important to say. Remember that AdCom members are overwhelmed with the volume of applications they must read. They will not appreciate reading an additional 500-word essay unless it really makes a big difference to your application.

So how important does information have to be for you to write this essay? This depends in part upon what the phrasing of the essay question implies about AdCom's attitude towards it. The former example "if there is anything additional…" suggests that anything relatively interesting about your candidacy that you have not addressed elsewhere could be added here. The latter phrasing, which mentions "extenuating circumstances," means that you had better not write this essay unless you really have significant extenuating circumstances you need to explain. Appropriate "extenuating" circumstances include:

> *Remember that AdCom members are overwhelmed with the volume of applications they must read. They will not appreciate reading an additional 500-word essay unless it really makes a big difference to your application.*

- Low scores: If your GMAT, TOEFL or undergraduate scores do not represent your abilities, you should explain so here. For example: "I want to address my low grades during my junior and senior years of college. My father was seriously injured in a traffic accident and in addition to my academics and job search, I was coping with emotional trauma and working 20 hours a week to help support my family."

- Career gap: If you have a gap in your career of more than about 2 months, you should explain the reason and what you did with the time. For example: "I was laid off at the end of 2008. I spent the next 3 months interviewing for new jobs, only to find that none were forthcoming. Therefore, in early 2009, I founded MathBlast, a small non-profit where I helped disadvantaged children learn mathematics."

- Recommendations: If you cannot have your current supervisor write a recommendation letter for you, you must explain why in this essay. For example: "Because I only started at my current

job a month prior to writing this application, I do not believe my current supervisor can write an accurate recommendation letter. Therefore, I have asked my former supervisor to write the letter, instead."

You should not write an "extra" essay if you just want to tell the ABC AdCom about your personal philosophy of learning or how you learned about the meaning of life during your cruise to the Greek islands last summer.

Recommendation Letters: Laser Guided Support for Your Application

Recommendation letters are a crucial part of your application, and if handled correctly, can help you present a much more convincing argument for your admission. However, if they are not well handled, they may either have no impact on your candidacy or even detract from it.

A good recommendation letter will have the following characteristics:

- *A strong relationship:* Your recommender must be someone with a real relationship to you. In fact, most recommendation letter forms provided by AdCom begin by asking the recommender to detail their relationship to you. Direct, day-to-day, substantial interaction over an extended period of time counts as a good relationship. Merely working at the same company does not. The purpose of the recommendation letter is to provide a third person's detailed observations about you, and that person's perspectives will not have any weight with AdCom if they do not have a solid relationship with you.

- *High levels of detail and insight:* A recommendation letter that uses a lot of positive adjectives about you without giving concrete and highly detailed examples of how you deserve those adjectives is worthless. A recommendation letter that simply repeats information available elsewhere in your application – especially information apparent from your resume – is also worthless. Your recommender must describe very detailed examples of your work, personality and decision-making, in a way that provides new insight into you as a person, and that is not available from your resume and essays.

- *A defined purpose within the context of your overall application:* Your recommendation letter should be designed as a part of your whole application package. That means it has to be consistent with your Admission Case. If your Admission Case is about your desire to reform the banking sector and your recommender talks about your interest in becoming a management consultant, you are in trouble. As much as possible, your recommendation letter should also address qualities from the 3Cs model a) where you appear weak, or b) that you have not

addressed elsewhere in the application. For example, if you got a poor quantitative score on your GMAT, try to have a recommender talk about your high quality work on a project with a strong quantitative or analytical component to make you look stronger along the intellect quality. If you have not talked about your teamwork, you should try to find a recommender who can talk about that time you put together a cross-disciplinary team to improve R&D's communication with marketing.

Choosing recommenders

As described briefly several times earlier in this guide, you should aim to use recommendation letters to give testimony about your abilities in qualities where you believe you have not been able to provide evidence adequate to represent your true abilities. These problem areas should be evident to you after you have gone through the self-evaluation and mapping exercises above. For example, if you think you have great innovation skills but simply could not find room in your essays to talk about innovation, you should try to get one of your recommenders to provide a specific example of your innovation in action.

However, remember that AdCom does not expect or even want you to be perfect. You do not need to get recommenders to attest to your excellence in every area where you have not elsewhere been able to provide evidence of top-notch skills. You are, after all, applying to business school in order to improve yourself, so you need to admit you have some room for improvement.

> *Many candidates make the fallacious and sometimes fatal assumption that the higher the status of the recommender the more value his or her recommendation has.*

A good specific example of a quality will be a detailed description of an instance where you demonstrated that quality while working closely with or under the recommender. The recommender should be able to describe the initial situation, your approach to resolving it, and the outcome, and also provide their personal insight into what this demonstrates about you as a person or employee.

Note that because most schools provide detailed forms for recommenders to fill, the recommender cannot simply write a paragraph or two about this instance. They will have to write about this instance within the constraints of the letter form, and they will have to complete other parts of the form that have nothing to do with this instance. So if you have the perfect recommender in mind to write about your innovation, consider where on the form it is most appropriate for them to touch on this subject, and think about what you would like them to write (and what they are likely to write whether you like it or not) in the other areas of the form.

Many candidates make the fallacious and sometimes fatal assumption that the higher the status of the recommender, the more value his or her recommendation has. This fallacy is especially common among applicants from Asian countries. Let us be entirely clear: the seniority of the recommender is not critically important. The most important qualities that a recommender can have correspond to the characteristics of a good recommendation letter listed above. That means, the recommender must have a strong relationship with you, must be willing and able to talk about you with detail and insight, and must be cooperative enough with you to write a letter that focuses on whatever you ask them to focus on.

Therefore, it is much better to submit a recommendation letter from a direct supervisor who can speak about you in detail based on his two years of working with you on a day-to-day basis than it is to submit a letter from the CEO of a Fortune 500 company if that CEO does not have an extensive working relationship with you.

Typically, most schools will ask for two recommendations, and some will give you the option of submitting a third. Ideally, the first two letters will come from people you have a professional relationship with. If you have the option of submitting a third letter, you have a certain amount of freedom as to who you pick, as long as you have a clear purpose for doing so.

One of the two obligatory recommendation letters should be from your current direct supervisor. If you do not submit a letter from your current direct supervisor, this omission will raise questions about your work performance in your current job. In such a case, you should explain why (likely in the "optional" extra essay described above). Acceptable reasons for not including a letter from your current direct supervisor include that you recently moved to your current position and your current supervisor does not yet know you well enough to write a recommendation or that your company is not supportive of its staff applying to MBA programs and to ask your supervisor for a recommendation would put you at risk of being fired.

Your second professional recommendation letter can come from someone else with a professional relationship with you. Other good professional sources of recommendation letters are past supervisors, mentors within your company, clients with whom you've worked closely, and (depending on the school to which you're applying) colleagues of equal rank.

When you have the option of submitting a third letter, as with the "optional" extra essay discussed above, you should only include this item if you have a very good reason to do so. For example, it's probably not worthwhile to submit a third recommendation written by a third supervisor/colleague that addresses your professional skills. As we have discussed earlier, sometimes including gratuitous information in your application can actually harm your chances of admission: AdCom members are overwhelmed with reading applications and can get annoyed at applicants who include additional or

optional information without a good reason. But if there is an aspect of your life that is important to you and where you are accomplished – perhaps you have extensive community service leadership experience – it may be valuable to include a recommendation letter from someone who can comment on that aspect of your life.

There are certain people who do not make good recommenders. You should be careful about including recommendation letters from college professors. While you may have had a great relationship with a professor, this will not necessarily impress AdCom members, who do not always see professors as a reliable source of information on how you function in the real world. If you do accept a professorial recommendation, it should be your third letter and there should be a strong reason for it – e.g., the professor was an advisor to you in some very substantial activity you participated in outside of the classroom, such as organizing an international conference. In such a situation, the professor is talking more about your leadership and management skills than your academic performance. Finally, it is never acceptable to include recommendation letters from family members, and recommendations from family friends may not be take seriously by AdCom.

Recommender fatigue

> **Recommendation letters often become the limiting factor on the number of schools you can apply to.**

Most schools provide a customized – and lengthy – recommendation letter form that your recommender must fill out. Because these forms differ between schools, your recommender will have to write a separate letter for each school to which you apply. Interestingly, this means that recommendation letters often become the limiting factor on the number of schools you can apply to. If you are hard-working enough, you can write essays for 10 schools. But it's unlikely that you can get your recommenders to do a good job on recommendations for more than 4 or 5 schools.

The do-it-yourself approach and its problems

Of course, this limiting factor does not exist if your recommender asks that you write your recommendation letters yourself. Strictly speaking, it is unethical for you to do so, and if your recommender refuses to write the letter him or herself, you must find another recommender. In reality, especially in countries where English is not the native tongue, it is a widespread phenomenon for applicants to draft their own recommendations and submit them to their recommenders for review and signing.

While the chance to write your own recommendation letter may seem like a great opportunity, it actually poses a few practical problems (in addition to ethical problems). Recommendation letters

should show a different person's perspective on you, and be written in a different person's voice. It can actually be quite difficult to write about yourself as another person would, and to make the style of the letter different from your own writing style. (AdCom members may notice if your essays and all your recommendation letters sound as though they were written by one person due to their style, diction, and other characteristics.)

> **While the chance to write your own recommendation letter may seem like a great opportunity, it actually poses a few practical problems.**

An ideal strategy

It is not at all unethical to suggest to your recommender specific topics that they mention about you. This fact suggests a good strategy for avoiding too much recommender fatigue while avoiding the ethical and practical problems of the DIY approach. For each school, provide your recommender a detailed outline of what you would like them to write about, in the format of that school's recommendation letter form. This tactic reduces much of the writing burden faced by the recommender, while ensuring that they write good letters customized to each school's requirements. Yet it still forces them to write a final version of the letter in their own voice. Discuss with your recommenders whether this strategy is acceptable to them.

If they still want to avoid such a large writing burden, you can consider having a third party with more time and/or better English writing skills than the recommender stepping in to help. This third party can take care of the bulk of the writing work, closely supervised by the recommender.

Working with recommenders

Naturally, you should approach your recommenders well before the deadline for your application deadline. Remember that even the most supportive recommender is going to be very busy with their own responsibilities, and the lengthy process of writing 4 or 5 recommendation letters for you will never be a top priority for them. It is easy for them to neglect or even forget about your letters. And even one missing recommendation letter is sometimes reason enough for AdCom to refuse to read your application. You should start talking to your recommenders 3 months before deadlines, and check up on their progress regularly enough that you can remain on top of things – but not so regularly that you annoy them!

When you talk to the recommender about the recommendation letter, present them with your suggestions about what they might want to write about during the letter. Depending on the recommender and your relationship with him or her, you may just want to mention the one or two key things you'd like them to cover, and leave the rest up to them, or provide detailed suggestions for each

part of the letter form. Once the recommender has received your suggestions, he or she may simply proceed to write the letter, or may ask for more input from you.

As the recommender writes the letters, you may want to discreetly inquire as to whether they would like someone to help him or her proofread the letters for style and grammar. This can be any third party with good English writing skills. Some recommenders may find this step unnecessary or inappropriate, but some will be happy to have a third party ensure that the letter they submit on your behalf is well polished.

Interviews: A Chance to Take the Initiative

If your written application is well-received by AdCom, they will probably invite you for an interview. Interviews rely on quite different skill sets than written applications – many very effective writers are not great interviewers, and vice-versa. Luckily, because interviews are usually only offered to candidates who have passed the initial screening of written applications, it makes sense to only start preparing for interviews after submitting your written applications. So there is no need to overwhelm yourself by learning how to improve your written application and your interviewing skills at the same time.

> *Interviews rely on quite different skill sets than written applications.*

A typical B-school interview lasts about 30-40 minutes in total. The first 2 minutes are spent on greetings. Then there is a roughly 20 to 30 minute period where the interviewer asks questions of you. Then you are normally offered about 5 minutes to ask questions of the interviewer. Finally, the last 3 minutes are used to summarize the interview, explain the next steps, and say your goodbyes. Some interviewers will stick to this schedule very tightly, while others will be less disciplined about time management.

Different kinds of interviews

There are three major ways along which interviews vary: the choice of an alumnus or AdCom member, the information the interviewer has about you prior to the interviewer, and the medium over which the interview takes place.

The first is the *AdCom/alumnus choice*. Most applicants, especially those applying from overseas, will face a choice of interviewing with a local alumnus (a term into which we group current students), or of interviewing with an AdCom member. (Many major schools' AdComs make interview trips through

major cities around the world.) There is often a significant difference in the two types of interviews. Generally speaking, AdCom members will have an extremely clear idea of what information they want from the applicant, and will run the interview in a highly structured way according to a set schedule. Some applicants come out of their AdCom interviews thinking that the interviewer moved through the interview at a pace that was hard to keep up with, or were assertive and direct enough to border on being rude. Alumni interviews, on the other hand, are relatively unpredictable. While AdCom tries to standardize alumni interviews by providing a certain amount of training to alumni interviewers, alumni interviewers tend to run their interviews in a much less structured manner. Despite their best intentions, they also face a number of distractions arising from their own jobs that can directly affect interviews, so they may not have even had time to read your resume before conducting the interview. Alumni interviews can cover almost any topic, can be fairly unstructured, and occasionally can be interrupted by urgent demands on the interviewer's time. But they also tend to be more conversational and slower paced than AdCom interviews, and are therefore easier for the applicant to direct in the direction he or she wants.

A final note is that while AdCom makes an effort to weigh alumni interviews equally with AdCom interviews when making final acceptance decisions, in some cases AdCom interviews can carry more weight. Why? First, because alumni interviewers do not always conduct interviews, or write interview reports, exactly as AdCom likes, AdCom may not receive all of the information it wants from an alumni interviewer, which will invariably make your interview have less weight. Moreover, if there is a vote among AdCom members about which of two applicants to accept, one of whom has an AdCom interviewer advocating for them, and the other of whom has a piece of paper from a distant alumni supporting them, it stands to reason that the applicant with the AdCom advocate will have an advantage.

The **interviewer's preparation** is another major differentiator among interviews. Some schools will provide the interviewer with all of an applicant's written application materials prior to the interview, and the interviewer may ask specific questions about the applicant's essays, undergraduate coursework, etc. Harvard is an example of a school that gives interviewers full access to all information. Most schools, however, limit the interviewer to much less, often only allowing them to read the applicant's resume. The less information the interviewer has about you prior to the interview, the more general their questions will be and the easier it will be for you to direct the interview in whatever direction you want. The more information the interviewer has, the more specific their questions, the more limited your possible responses, and the less room you will have to determine the direction of the discussion. Clearly, it is important to understand what information the interviewer has seen about you prior to preparing for the interview. It's not good to walk into an interview prepared to talk about your resume, but to face specific, unexpected questions about essays you wrote 8 weeks ago and don't clearly remember.

Real World Example

One applicant had very different experiences in an alumnus interview at a school that only provided resumes to interviewers, and an AdCom interview with a school that provided the full written application to interviewers.

The alumnus interviewer greeted the applicant, picked up a pen and said "let's make this easy for both of us. Just give me 3 bullet points you want me to tell AdCom about you. Don't even bother me with lots of description and evidence; I just want the bullets." After the surprised applicant listed three bullet points with a minimal explanation of each, the interviewer leaned back in his chair and started talking about the best annual campus parties the applicant should attend if admitted.

The AdCom interviewer started the interview by apologizing for her impending rudeness. She then asked the applicant pointed questions about his written application, frequently interrupting him halfway through a response with another question. After exactly 15 minutes the interviewer cut off the applicant in mid-sentence and explained that the time limit for the interview was over.

Whether you would find the first or the second of these interviews more stressful depends on your personality. But in either case, careful preparation prior to the interview, and a sense of humor during the interview, would be very valuable.

Finally, the **medium** of the interview is an important factor. Most interviews are conducted face-to-face, so that the two parties can interact fully, not only by talking but also with facial expressions, body language, and eye contact. In some cases, a face-to-face interview is impossible and the school offers a phone interview instead. Phone interviews are considered by many interviewers to provide a less complete form of communication, as only talking (and not any form of visual communication) is possible. Some applicants have tried to take advantage of the privacy afforded by phone interviews to try to answer as many interview questions as possible by reading from written scripts. This is usually a bad idea, because unless you are a skilled actor, you will not sound natural when reading aloud. In order to regain some amount of visual communication in remote interviews, some schools have begun using video conferences instead of phone interviews. Video conferences go part way to allowing the same complete form of communication that is possible in a face-to-face interview, but are still not the same. For example, it is hard to achieve eye contact in a video conference because the video camera you're speaking into is often not well aligned with your monitor.

What the interviewer wants

Interviewers are trying to get a fairly full picture of the applicant as a complete person. That means they want to have a real conversation with you, about a range of topics. They want you to be polite, but also friendly. You should adhere to basic interview etiquette – dress formally, shake hands, offer polite greetings, wait to be offered a seat, maintain good eye contact and an upright posture, and bring extra resumes in case the interviewer forgot his copy. But you do not need to be extremely formal and stiff. You can smile and laugh, you don't need to sit at attention with your hands in your lap, and you can portray yourself as a normal human being, not a robotic business machine.

Note that the interviewer, despite having the job of objectively evaluating you, probably has a positive attitude towards you. She knows you are nervous, and empathizes with you because either she is an AdCom member who has seen a thousand nervous applicants before, or because she was once a nervous applicant just like you. Unless she is unusually sadistic, she does not like to reject people and would prefer to see you have a great interview, rather than observe as you fail miserably. So, don't psyche yourself out if you make a small mistake – the interviewer will be forgiving if you can recover and continue.

> **One of the interviewer's main goals is to see if your Mission Statement makes sense – to you.**

Nevertheless, the interviewer has a clear agenda about what she wants to learn. There are specific qualities that most interviewers will focus on, as illustrated in the mapping charts at the beginning of this section. Generally, interviewers are primarily focused on goals, progress, effort and communication. As one interviewer for a top business school emphasized, one of the interviewer's major goals is to see if your Mission Statement makes sense – to you. If you wrote essays about goals that you made up to sound impressive to a school that you just want to attend for the status, you're probably going to have trouble looking an interviewer in the eye and explaining why those goals and this school are important to you. A lot of applicants whose essays look great fail the interview within the first few minutes because they simply can't lie convincingly in person to an interviewer who's learned to detect lies during the process of evaluating hundreds or thousands of previous candidates. The solution to this problem is not to learn acting skills. It is to choose goals that are meaningful to you.

Interviewers will also frequently take a strong interest in leadership, teamwork, involvement, maturity, and uniqueness. Depending on the school, the interviewer, and the applicant, the interviewer may exclude one or more of these and/or include one or more of several other qualities. However, it is rare that an interviewer will ask questions about your intellect.

The interviewer will expect you to have very coherent and logical prepared answers to questions along the lines of the qualities listed above. You will need a very clear and detailed reason why you prefer the

particular school the interviewer represents. He or she will also expect you to be able to jump to other topics and talk about them in a way that, while perhaps not as organized and polished as your prepared answer, is coherent and makes sense given your goals and background.

The interviewer will also expect you to show your effort by having some very good questions about his or her school. Good questions are *not* "can you tell me how many finance electives you offer?" or "what percentage of your students get consulting internships?" These questions can be answered by online research. Don't waste the interviewer's time by asking them to repeat information you should already have. Good questions address issues that are not covered in online catalogues. The best questions also imply that you have already taken the effort to conduct extensive online research about the school, and preferably have also talked to current students or alumni. With that research behind you, you have some detailed or personal questions that you'd like the interviewer's personal insight into.

> *You should tailor your questions to the interviewer.*

You should tailor your questions to the interviewer. If the interviewer is an AdCom member, you can ask very specific questions about school policies and programs, for example:

- What specific measures is the career placement office taking to help students compete for jobs in the current economic downturn?

- I've noticed that school X has recently launched a new program on international leadership. Overall I like your school better, but I haven't found anything quite the same at your school. Are there any plans to open a similar program, or are do you have suggestions about where I could get similar training at your school?

- I've noticed Professor Y, who is in the statistics department of your university but who is not associated with the MBA program, is doing some very interesting research into applied behavioral economics theory and stock pricing that I think would be valuable to my future career plans. I haven't been able to learn from your website whether there's any way I could work with him as a research assistant for MBA credit. Do you know if it's possible?

If your interviewer is a current student or recent graduate, they will probably not have a good command of detailed questions like the above. You can try asking more personal questions about their experience:

- What are the skills or resources you gained from your MBA that you use most often in your day-to-day work?

- How much support have your recently laid off classmates received from the alumni network and office of career services during the current market downturn?

- I have a lot of interest in the politics/MBA joint degree program. Did you have any friends who participated in that program? If so, how did they balance the workload, and how did they plan to use the joint degrees in the future?

If you are talking to a more senior alumnus, it can be a little harder to connect with questions like those above because the school has probably evolved greatly since they attended. You can start by asking relatively broad questions that ask them to look back over their career, and ask appropriate, specific follow-up questions based on their initial responses:

- Over the past 15 years, how has your MBA been valuable to your career development?

- How involved do you stay with the alumni network, and how has it been valuable to you?

- What do you wish you had known before you began your MBA?

Notice that all of the questions above, while they touch on very different topics, are open questions that the interviewer cannot simply answer with a yes or no. If possible, turn your questions into short back and forth dialogues. If you ask a question and the interviewer responds, listen carefully to his or her response and ask appropriate follow-up questions. This will demonstrate your high level interest in their responses.

Finally it is important to note that MBA interviews differ from job interviews in an important aspect: the interviewer is not going to be working with you. In a job interview, an unspoken question in the forefront of the interviewer's mind is usually "do I like this person? Do I want to work overtime with her at 2AM in the morning?" This question adds an extra layer of subjectivity to job interviews. But this question is not necessarily urgently important to MBA interviewers, who are aware they will probably never see you again.

Steering interviews

It is important to understand that your role in an interview is not simply to answer questions posed by the interviewer, and then ask a few pre-prepared questions to demonstrate your interest in the school. If this is your approach to interviews, you may not be able to give your strongest performance. Why not? Because the interviewer might not ask questions that directly address the most impressive aspects of your candidacy. Instead of merely reacting to questions, you should arrive at the interview with a clear agenda of what you want to talk about, and seek to steer the discussion to meet your agenda.

> *Your role in an interview is not simply to answer questions posed by the interviewer.*

Consider your agenda the same way you might if you were representing your company at the Q&A session of a press event. You would certainly go into such a session with a clear idea of what points you wanted to get across, regardless of what questions you were asked. Your interview agenda should be 2 to 4 major bullet points about yourself you want to be sure you discuss with the interviewer. The purpose of these bullet points is very clear. After your interview is over, your interviewer will fill out an evaluation form in which he describes your performance to AdCom. You literally want your interviewer to note down your agenda bullet points on his or her evaluation form. You will not always be able to talk about all of your agenda bullet points, but if you come to your interviews properly prepared, you should be able to address at least some of them in each interview.

Where do you get your agenda bullet points from? Return to your Mission Statement and Admission Case and pick out a few key points you want to stress in the interview. As you do so, remember that the interviewer is going to be particularly interested in certain qualities (as listed above), and you should pick points that reflect this fact.

Raising your bullet points during the interview can be a bit of an art. The key skill is to take a question that is tangentially related to one of your bullet points and respond in a way that appears to address the original question, but steers the discussion to your bullet point, and to make this transition without being blatantly obvious about it. This will require an ability to think on your feet, as well as good active listening skills to read the reaction of the interviewer even as you speak.

For example, imagine that one of your bullet points is that you are a very strong communicator, especially in intercultural situations. If your interviewer asks you about your hobbies, directly address the question by talking about how you like to travel. But after a sentence or two about travel, you can stick in a couple of sentences about how your greatest takeaway from travel is an ability to communicate in intercultural situations, and that this skill has been a great benefit to your personal and professional life. At this point, you will have to read and react to subtle cues from the interviewer, to decide whether or not you want to continue talking about your communication bullet point. Look at his or her body language, listen for any responses, check whether they are making eye contact, and so on. If you believe the interviewer is interested in your tangential remarks about communication, continue on with one or two examples. If the interviewer looks bored, confused or annoyed at your digression, you may want to jump back to talking about travel or other hobbies.

Steering a conversation in a way that lets you cover your bullet points without seemingly ignoring the interviewer's questions is an entire skill of its own that takes time to practice. (In fact, some business

schools offer courses in exactly this skill, intended for use in public relations jobs.) This skill is one that is best practiced during the mock interview practice sessions described below.

How to prepare for interviews

Walking into an interview without doing considerable preparation is an easy way to seriously damage your application. There are two major steps to preparing for an interview. The first is to prepare for common interview questions, ideally by writing down answers that you can rehearse on your own. The second is to conduct live interview practice.

Begin by composing answers to common interview questions. Most typical interview questions are quite similar to the model essay questions above. Interviewers will ask questions meant to test you along a similar array of qualities. So return to the model essay questions and begin crafting responses. Note that your responses should generally have the same basic structure as essays in terms of setup, action and analysis.

However, you cannot recite a complete essay in response to every question – at normal talking speed, reciting a full essay will take too long and the interviewer will get bored and lose track of what you're saying. For most questions, you should prepare a response that takes about one to two minutes to say at normal talking speed (native speakers speaking at normal speed generally speak 100 words a minute). This means it has to be shorter and simpler than an application essay. If the interviewer is

Steering a conversation in a way that lets you cover your bullet points without seemingly ignoring the interviewer's questions is an entire skill of its own that takes time to practice.

curious about your initial response, he will ask follow up questions that direct you to explain the details you left out.

It is also usually not a good idea to memorize responses verbatim. Even if you have the ability and time to do so, your performance during the interview will probably seem unnatural and off-putting, unless you are a trained actor. You are much better off setting up bullet point outlines of your answers, memorizing the bullet points, and then practicing speaking naturally based on the bullet points you've memorized.

Mapping each response to specific qualities is not a perfectly straightforward task, as you do not know which questions will eventually be asked. For example, if you prepare 10 responses to likely questions, each covering one quality, and in the end you are only asked 4 questions, you will have completely ignored 6 qualities. The best strategy in this situation is to think of a few stories that can be used to respond to each quality, and a few qualities that can be covered in every story. So if your interviewer asks you about leadership, you can respond with a story that also addresses innovation and

management. If the interviewer then asks for further examples of your management experience, you can give a response that also touches upon your communication and teamwork qualities.

Also, as you prepare your responses, consider the agenda bullet points described above. As many responses as possible should either contain content relative to one of your bullet points, or at least offer an easy transition to one of your bullet points.

> *You should devote special attention to preparing for the question that most interviews start with – a question about your goals.*

You should devote special attention to preparing for the question that most interviews start with – a question about your goals. This initial question is basically a request for your Mission Statement – what you want to achieve in life, why, what you have already done to get there, what skills you need to add, how you will add those skills, and how the MBA is a part of this process. Develop a 2 to 3 minute, highly organized response to this question that is based on your Mission Statement.

It is very important to answer this question well. A good answer provides a clear rationale why you want admission, and provides structure for the rest of the interview. A poor answer may confuse the interviewer and lead him to spend several minutes of valuable interview time clarifying what your goals are and why you need an MBA.

Note that this question can be asked in many different ways: "Why do you want an MBA?" "What are your career goals?" "Please give me some background about yourself." "Walk me through your resume." It is easy to adapt your response to the particular phrasing your interviewer uses. For example, if he says "walk me through your resume," you can start by saying "Sure. Well, my resume really reflects my long term career goals of X and Y. I developed these goals because…" Then you can start going through the education and work experience on your resume within the context of the goals you just outlined, which will make your response much easier for the interviewer to digest and react to.

Once you have prepared written outlines of your responses, rehearse them out loud, and make sure you can cover them in about the right amount of time. If they're too long, make some tough decisions to shorten them – remember that if the interviewer feels any important details are missing, he will simply ask you, and you will have a chance to add back the parts you omitted during your initial response.

When you feel you are ready, conduct some mock interviews. To do mock interviews, you need a partner who will play the role of the interviewer. An effective way to find a partner is to ask other MBA applicants. Any serious applicant will be happy to help you practice if you help them practice in return. Mock interviews should, as much as possible, mimic a real interview. If at all possible, find a quiet, secluded location where you will not be disturbed and practice every step of the interview, from the

initial handshake to the final goodbyes. (Note that the person playing the interviewer does not have to provide answers to the questions asked by the person playing the applicant.) Immediately after the mock interview is over, the person who played the interviewer should give critical feedback to the person who played the applicant, ranging from the structure, content and length of his responses to his body language and eye contact.

If possible, record your mock interview sessions with a video camera and watch the recordings to see how you look. You may find that in an interview setting you make too little eye contact, or you tend to lean over to your right instead of sitting up straight, or that you speak too quickly to be easily understood. These are all imperfections that you can correct with practice.

Application Timelines

The timelines below are general and high level guidelines for how to plan and use your time during the MBA application process. Both plans show dates for applying to Round 1 deadlines at American programs, which begin in early October (in most cases). If you plan to apply to Round 2 or Round 3, you can simply offset the entire schedule by a few months to create an appropriate plan for yourself.

12 Month Application Timeline

Jan	Make initial Application Strategy and Self Assessment
Feb	Begin addressing weaknesses
Mar	Study, research schools
Apr	Complete exams, research schools
May	Study, research schools
Jun	Retake exams if necessary, finalize Application Strategy
Jul	Create Communication Strategy, solicit recommendations
Aug	Perform mapping, begin writing applications
Sep	Continue writing applications
Oct	SUBMIT APPLICATIONS
Nov	Inquire about official undergraduate transcripts, practice interviews
Dec	Interviews

The first timeline is for applicants who give themselves twelve months to complete the entire process from initial planning to final interviews. These applicants begin in January of the year they will apply in, and follow the process through December. During the first 9 months, they plan their applications, take steps to address any obvious weaknesses in their candidacies, research interesting schools, take exams, find recommenders, and write the applications. Because they have allowed themselves ample time, they can easily retake the GMAT or TOEFL if their first scores are unsatisfactory, and are probably flexible enough to adjust if some unexpected crisis – such as an urgent project at work – suddenly cuts into their schedule. During the remaining 3 months, they submit their applications, begin the process of obtaining official college transcripts, and prepare for and conduct interviews.

9 Month Application Timeline

Apr	Make initial Application Strategy and Self-Assessment
May	Study, research schools, begin addressing weaknesses
Jun	Take exams, research schools
Jul	Retake exams if necessary, research schools
Aug	Finalize strategy, perform mapping, solicit recommendations
Sep	Write applications
Oct	SUBMIT APPLICATIONS
Nov	Inquire about official undergraduate transcripts, practice interviews
Dec	Interviews

The second timeline shows a shorter nine month timeline, for an applicant who starts in mid spring. These applicants do not have so much time to be flexible. They must rush through preparation. If they perform poorly on an exam, they might just barely be able to squeeze in another test date before they have to start writing essays. But if anything else goes wrong – illness, an unexpectedly heavy workload, etc. – they will have a great deal of difficulty meeting their application deadlines.

There are a few terms in these timelines that bear some explanation:

- ***Research schools:*** In terms of research, you should start with simple sources, such as the rankings reports published by several media companies, and school websites. As you begin to narrow down the list of schools you'd like to apply to, you should begin seeking more first-person research opportunities. These opportunities include formal school presentations, "coffee chats," meetings with alumni, and even campus visits. Research will help you learn information that will help you decide which schools you'd like to attend. Just as importantly, remember that showing effort is an important aspect of your application; doing thorough, in-person research is an excellent way of demonstrating effort.

- ***Address weaknesses:*** As discussed in the Application Strategy and Communication Strategy sections of this book, as a part of your MBA application, you should assess skills, knowledge and resources you need to gain to achieve your career goals, and also areas of weakness that might be apparent to AdCom. As you identify these developmental needs, you should think about what you can do to address them before you apply. It makes you look like a much stronger applicant if you can say "I know I'm weak in fundamental business skills like accounting and finance, and that's why I've enrolled in 3 business courses at my local college," rather than saying "I am weak at fundamental business skills and I hope your school will help me address these weaknesses." Note that addressing these weaknesses is usually a lengthy process that will continue throughout your application and possibly right up to the beginning of classes.

Frequently Asked Questions

Can my score of XX on the GMAT get me into school YY?

The short answer is "It's hard to say." AdCom is going to look at a whole range of things in your application – what we have tried to address with the 3Cs model – of which your GMAT score is merely one. There is a tendency among applicants to focus too much on their GMAT scores, as this is the single most easily measured and compared metric. This tendency is especially strong in Asia, where test scores are often the only or the overwhelmingly most important factor in deciding undergraduate school admissions.

That said, the GMAT score is undeniably important to your application, as AdCom uses it to evaluate your intellect and ability to complete the academic component of your MBA. You can use the average GMAT score as a guideline. But don't get dissuaded if you are a bit below the average – by definition, half of the students who gain admission are also below the average. A better guideline is the 80% range; the range of scores in which the middle 80% of students reside. If you are within this 80% range, you certainly won't be disqualified based on your GMAT score. However, if you are below the 80% range, you will have to make up for this with compelling strengths and development potential in other areas of your application. Moreover, some schools publish a minimum admissible score. If you are below the minimum score, you cannot be admitted no matter how good the rest of your application is.

You can help to mitigate the disadvantage of having a relatively low GMAT score by taking steps that show AdCom you want to improve yourself. For example, if you did poorly in the quantitative section, enroll in an algebra and calculus course at a local college, and mention this in your application. Remember that AdCom members usually respect applicants who recognize their own weaknesses and take steps to improve on them.

I am weak in math, and this weakness is reflected in my GPA and GMAT scores. What can I do?

Math, quantitative, and analytical skills are all important to AdCom. This is because MBA coursework is highly quantitative, and also because typical post-MBA jobs are highly quantitative; an MBA student who is weak in math may not be able to complete the academic coursework in the MBA, and even if he does graduate, might have a hard time getting retained and promoted by an employer. However, there are a number of steps you can take to address a weakness in math.

First, ensure that your proposed major and career goals are realistic given your weakness. For example, claiming that you want to major in finance and go into investment banking after graduation won't sound realistic. You might be better off focusing on areas like marketing, corporate strategy, entrepreneurism, etc.

Second, show you are making efforts to improve your quantitative skills. Enroll in quantitative courses at a local college or ask for some quantitative assignments at work.

Third, try to find a recommendation letter writer who can write about a specific instance at work where you showed an ability to perform quantitative work. If you're not a math whiz in the classroom but you can get things done when it really counts in the real world, AdCom may be quite happy with you.

Ultimately, you do not need to convince AdCom that you are a math genius. You merely have to convince them that you have or are developing quantitative skills sufficient to get you through the MBA and into the career you want.

I work in an independent sales job where I have no direct reports. How can I talk about qualities like leadership?

It is important to recognize that AdCom recognizes leadership as a quality that is demonstrated through actions, not by a job title. Thus, being "team leader" or "supervisor" of a 5 person team at work does not provide much evidence of your leadership ability. In fact, AdCom is likely to be more impressed by leadership roles you've taken on without a formal title or authority, because when you are in a formal leadership role, people may be following you merely because of your title or authority, rather than because of your innate leadership ability.

So, think about things you've done at work, back in university, or in other activities where you've influenced other people to act in ways that they otherwise would not. Perhaps in your role as a salesperson you do not lead anyone, but at work you informally led a group of coworkers to propose a new evaluation and compensation program to management. That's a great leadership experience. Or maybe you were elected to lead a large student organization back in university – that's also fair game for leadership.

Finally, remember that you're applying for an MBA because you want to improve yourself. Maybe leadership is one of the areas you need to improve. You can actually strengthen your case for admission by speaking about your interest and native ability, but limited personal experience, in leadership, and your belief that the specific leadership programs available at XYZ's MBA program can help you fully develop your leadership skills.

I have a humanities/engineering background and my previous experience gives me almost no exposure to business or to business concepts like accounting, marketing, management, etc. What can I do?

A need to learn business skills like accounting, management, etc., while it seems like a weakness, also can be presented as a compelling explanation for why you want to attend an MBA program. The key is to couch this explanation in the right context, because if you seem completely clueless about business concepts AdCom may think you are not serious or well-prepared enough.

If you are weak in these areas, you should show you are serious about business by enrolling in some courses at a local university. You can sign up for accounting, finance, marketing, etc. courses relatively easily.

You will also need to ensure that your career goals are very well thought out, so that it is clear to AdCom that despite your non-business background, you know what you want to do in business in the future. And make sure to champion how the skills you developed in your previous non-business roles are transferrable to business. Demonstrating that you are strong in several qualities makes this point implicitly, but don't be afraid to make this point explicitly.

Also, if you are currently working in an organization with several divisions, you can consider switching to another division. Perhaps you are an engineer and you have always worked in the R&D division, or you have a degree in communications and you have been in the PR division. Ask your managers if you can switch to a more front-line business division such as sales, marketing, strategy, etc. Many managers are more likely to allow this kind of inter-departmental jump if you justify it by explaining that you want to learn more about the workings of the whole organization so you can develop your career there.

I was accepted by these 2 schools, which one should I accept?

You should make your final school choice based on which school will have the most value in helping you meet your long term career goals. Some issues to consider when evaluating long term value include the school's overall reputation, its specific strengths in the fields you want to study and work in, and its recruiting relationships with the companies where you'd like to work after graduation.

Remember that an MBA is an investment that will be providing returns for 30 or 40 years. Do not make an investment with a smaller long term payoff to get some small benefit now. For example, while a partial scholarship may be an enticing way to save some money now, choosing a significantly better school without a scholarship will probably be better for you in the long run. Similarly, don't choose a school with less long term value because you prefer its climate, location, or similar features.

Also, don't get too caught up in the rankings game when choosing your school. There's really not much difference between the number 3 ranked school and the number 6 ranked school, and the rankings are likely to change in the next set of rankings anyway. However, there will be a real difference between the 3rd ranked school and the 13th ranked school, if not in the content of the education offered, then in the value of having the school's brand name on your resume for the rest of your career.

I was waitlisted. What should I do?

Unfortunately, there is often little you can do when waitlisted, which makes the waitlist experience extremely frustrating. Many schools have an explicit policy that any attempt to contact AdCom or provide additional information will actually *hurt* your chances of finally being accepted. Check the waitlist letter you received, or the school's website, to be sure what their policy is. If they state "please do not contact us," take their advice and do not contact them. They are not going to make an exception for you and you will simply be annoying them. Other schools say "please keep in touch with us by email every two or three weeks." In such a case, send a brief email every two or three weeks to reiterate your enthusiasm and to update the school on any significant changes to your candidacy (e.g., a new job).

In some cases, the school will request additional information from you, perhaps something like an additional recommendation letter. In this case, be sure to promptly reply with that information (and only that information).

I was rejected. What should I do?

Upon receiving rejection notification, immediately check the school's feedback policy. Every school has a different policy – for example, some offer no feedback to anyone, while others are willing to offer detailed feedback to the first 500 applicants who ask for it. Hearing from AdCom why they rejected you, while a potentially painful experience, can provide invaluable insight into how to improve your applications next year. Asking AdCom for feedback also signals that you are very serious about your application to that school and will not be discouraged by an initial failure.

If you can't get feedback, you will have to do your best to analyze why you were rejected. Do your best to objectively evaluate which parts of your application were probably weakest.

After compiling a list of reasons why you were rejected, the next step is to address these reasons. Some reasons may require you to go out and do something significant – maybe AdCom says they want you to have better domain skills and management skills. Addressing this may require a change in jobs or some significant commitments in your downtime. Or maybe you simply need to do a better job of presenting

AKAD MBA Application Guide
www.akadgroup.com

something that you already have. Perhaps your application did not convincingly show leadership and cooperation skills that you really have because you did a poor job of writing the relevant essays. Rather than seeking out new leadership and cooperation experiences, you can just do a better job of planning and writing your application next year.